Joss Whedon's Names

Other Works by Valerie Estelle Frankel

Henry Potty and the Pet Rock: An Unauthorized Harry Potter Parody

Henry Potty and the Deathly Paper Shortage: An Unauthorized Harry Potter Parody

Buffy and the Heroine's Journey

From Girl to Goddess: The Heroine's Journey in Myth and Legend

Katniss the Cattail: The Unauthorized Guide to Name and Symbols in The Hunger Games

The Many Faces of Katniss Everdeen: Exploring the Heroine of The Hunger Games

Harry Potter, Still Recruiting: An Inner Look at Harry Potter Fandom

Teaching with Harry Potter

An Unexpected Parody: The Unauthorized Spoof of The Hobbit Movie

Teaching with Harry Potter

Myths and Motifs in The Mortal Instruments

Winning the Game of Thrones: The Host of Characters and their Agendas

Winter is Coming: Symbols, Portents, and Hidden Meanings in A Game of Thrones

Bloodsuckers on the Bayou: The Myths, Symbols, and Tales Behind HBO's True Blood

The Girl's Guide to the Heroine's Journey

Choosing to be Insurgent or Allegiant: Symbols, Themes & Analysis of the Divergent Trilogy

Doctor Who and the Hero's Journey: The Doctor and Companions as Chosen Ones

Doctor Who: The What Where and How

Sherlock: Every Canon Reference You May Have Missed in BBC's Series 1-3

Women in Game of Thrones: Power, Conformity, and Resistance

Joss Whedon's Names

The Deeper Meanings behind *Buffy, Angel, Firefly, Dollhouse, Agents of S.H.I.E.L.D., Cabin in the Woods, The Avengers, Doctor Horrible, In Your Eyes,* Comics and More

Valerie Estelle Frankel

Joss Whedon's Names
by Valerie Estelle Frankel
Copyright © 2014 Valerie Estelle Frankel

ISBN-13: 978-0692216385 (LitCrit Press)
ISBN-10: 0692216383

Contents

Introduction

Many have noticed particular gems in the names of Joss Whedon. There's Jayne Cobb, stuck with a "girl's name." Mal, Latin for bad. Doctor Horrible, Captain Hammer, Penny and Moist. The beloved Buffy the Vampire Slayer, whose very name is a joke. Angel and Spike, Xander and Willow – the names overflow with meaning.

This book examines all the Whedon names, contrasting and cross-comparing. There are tropes of naming oneself for strong characters and drifting namelessly for weaker people. There are nature names for (mostly) Whedon's ladies: River, Skye, Dawn, Willow, Robin Wood, Sierra, Ivy, Iris, Dandelion, Lily, Jasmine, Saffron. There are superhero names, nicknames, aliases, hacker names, and NATO designations. There are allusions to literature, history, and myth. Word names are the most frequent from Pike to Faith to Glory to Echo to Serenity itself. Some are Puritan style (Patience Buckner, Jayne Cobb's mother Radiance, or the ridiculously named Fantastic Rample) while others emphasize their skills: Charles Gunn, Abigail Brand, The Siphon, Shepherd Book. There are the villains and heroes with Bible names: Simon Tam and Paul Ballard versus Caleb, Adam, Luke, Eve, and the chilling Dr. Mathias. There are many Daniels, Danas and Danielles, many Carls and Carolines, and most of all Williams and Wills. Comparing these for patterns, allusions, and clever winks to the audience reveals everything about Whedon's naming patterns as well as characters' hidden agendas.

For the five television shows, Whedon appears to have

named or co-named the major characters and many minor characters. Likewise, for his movies *In Your Eyes, Cabin in the Woods* and *Doctor Horrible,* the characters were thoroughly his. It's unlikely that he invented or named characters in his script treatments, but in his comic book runs, he added characters to the preexisting Marvel's *X-Men* and *Runaways* regulars. *The Avengers* gave him less of a chance, with many returning characters and an ensemble of comic-book superheroes needing screentime, but he added plenty to their universe through *Agents of S.H.I.E.L.D.. Alien: Resurrection* was his script and his characters, aside from the returning Ripley. His original comics from *Fray* to *Sugarshock* offer more intriguing names and characters, from Melaka Fray to Phil the Robot. Even when he doesn't invent or name a character, it's generally created by one of his co-producers, who share his delight in pop culture references and clever naming. In the DVD commentary of "Earshot," Jane Espenson says, "In general, if a line's really good, it tends to be his. It's remarkable how many times the writers get complimented on a line and it turns out to be one of Joss's." The same is true for names. As popular *Buffy* critic Rhonda V. Wilcox concludes, "One should never overlook the significance of naming and language in *Buffy*" ("Who Died and Made Her the Boss?" 8).·

The importance of naming is hardly a surprise for someone who named himself "Joss" (Chinese for lucky) from the more prosaic Joseph Hill Whedon. In fact, Joss Whedon and his wife Kai Cole named their son Arden and daughter Squire, continuing the exotic naming tradition.

Of course, there are no characters named Joss or Joseph or Hill. Even John is rare (whereas, other shows created a strong everyman hero named John Sheppard John Crichton, or John Sheridan). Jayne Cobb, Johner, and Joan (what Buffy names herself in "Tabula Rasa") are closest, though the Joss stand-ins generally have geeky nicknames: Wash, Topher, Fitz, and Xander. Jesse McNally, Xander's friend killed in the first episode, shares characteristics of both.

This book examines the original character names – not Wolverine or Thor but Buffy and her friends along with Darla, Harmony, and even Aphrodesia. After examining name meanings, name origins, and each name's impact on the character arc, the book moves to the next series: *Angel, Firefly/Serenity, Dollhouse, Agents of S.H.I.E.L.D.*, then the comics *Fray, Runaways, Sugarshock and X-Men* and the movies *Alien: Resurrection, The Cabin in the Woods, Doctor Horrible's Sing Along Blog,* and *In Your Eyes.* An appendix at the end cross-compares characters, sorting the names by similarity and origin.

Buffy the Vampire Slayer and *Angel*

While struggling through high school, Buffy battles vampires, because she's the chosen one. In the movie, she discovers her destiny and is kicked out of her L.A. high school. Her story continues as she finds herself at Sunnydale High with beloved friends, a mentor-librarian and a boyfriend who's a vampire. After she graduates, she continues through college and beyond as she discovers how to recreate the world into a place of true girl power.

After *Buffy*'s third season, Angel leaves for L.A. and starts a detective agency in his own spin-off. Cordelia joins him from *Buffy*, as does former watcher Wesley Wyndam-Pryce. With a few more allies, they battle demons and especially the evil law firm of Wolfram and Hart.

The Scoobies

Alexander "Xander" Lavelle Harris

Alexander is a popular American name, reminiscent of the great conqueror of worlds (who was also known for being unsubtle). This foreshadows a great future for Xander someday. His name means "defending men," and indeed, he's Buffy's defender and "cavalry" on occasion. Xander turns into a soldier in "Halloween" (B2.6), showing that he truly does have a tough guy inside him. He retains the training and power of command, which he uses on occasion thereafter.

According to Greek legend, the first Alexander was Paris, who absconded with Helen of Troy and destroyed all his family and friends with his love. Xander's romantic selfishness certainly throws his friends into chaos and creates the conflict of several episodes. Thanks to his betrayals, Buffy transforms into a rat while women fight over him, Buffy nearly kills Angel, Cordelia wishes Buffy had never come to Sunnydale, and Anya turns vengeance demon once more. If anyone is the Paris of the series, it's him.

At the same time, he calls himself Xander, an esoteric, even geeky version of the grandiose name, with the science-fiction "X" starting it off. Thus he sets himself up as described in the script: He is "bright, funny, and will one day be suave and handsome. Till that day arrives, he'll do the best he can with bright and funny" (*Buffy: The Script Book*). The first time we meet him, he's falling off his skateboard, and he goes through much of the series as comic relief, absent of the powers the other characters boast. Over time Xander "gradually acquires a sense of his own worth," Roz Kaveney explains in her essays ("She Saved the World, a Lot" 11). At the same time, he's the most "human" of the characters – someone for the audience to identify with, who strengthens his friends in times of emotional torment.

"Xander stands for Joss Whedon – and, again, for every normal person lost in a mad, mad world" (Wilcox, *Why Buffy Matters* 141). Whedon is known for creating stand-ins for himself, geeky goofy boys who are the immature best friend to the story's powerful women. He's the ordinary teen, the science fiction fan with a crush on Buffy – he's us. When Xander asks for an explanation "for those of us in our... audience who are me," he provides a bridge to understanding for us, the audience who are him.

"Xander is another name clearly launched by Whedon. When the series debuted in 1997, Xander was a rarity. By 1999, he was in the US Top 100, and he's gained quickly since" (appellationmountain). On the show, Xander's name stands out as unusual – when the team lose their memories in "Tabula Rasa" (B6.8), Willow calls him the standard "Alex." Xander wants to be called the more impressive and daring "Nighthawk" in "Dead Man's Party" (B3.2) and Sergeant Fury in the comics, but is always simply Xander (though by season seven, sometimes "Mr. Harris"). If a cool nickname is his goal, he never truly acquires one.

Like Xander, Lavelle is an unusual name. Meanings and uses vary widely, from a kingly household of Ireland to a surname and girl's name. Xander too is struggling for his place as he decides which identity he wishes for himself. The Irish meaning of Lavelle is "fond of movement or travel," while the French name comes from Laval, from Old French for "valley." So Xander is "from the valley" (or rather the dale, specifically Sunnydale) and also eager to go travel (as seen when he decides to backpack around the world, drifts through jobs, and finally joins Buffy in Scotland during the comics).

Harris, from "son of Harry," is one of the most common surnames in Britain. Thus he comes from traditional roots, even as he struggles to reinvent himself . It's a soundalike for the Arabic Haris, which means "Lion" or "Guardian" and heir, hinting that he is an heir to the Slayer legacy as well as Buffy's soldier and guardian. In Greek "alexo" means "to protect" or "to help," and he is Buffy's perpetual right hand, no matter the difficulty.

Xander may be named in homage to Zonker Harris, the stereotypical unfocused hippie from *Doonesbury*, though he grows far beyond his episode one role.

Anya Christina Emanuella Jenkins/Aud/Anyanka

> Some call this character "Aud," others "Anyanka." Throughout her elongated life and namesakes – Anya Emerson, vengeance demon, Mrs. Xander Harris, Mrs. Anya Christina Emanuella Jenkins Harris, Mrs. Anya lame-ass made up maiden name Harris – we have come to know her simply as Anya. (Francis)

Aud begins her story with an "odd" name emphasizing her oddness. "But it is worth remembering that her oddity started in innocence and goodwill, distorted by a choice to control" (Wilcox, *Why Buffy Matters* 55). Tellingly, the name means "deserted, empty" in Norwegian, heralding her lifelong struggle for the spouse, employer, job or even name that will give her a stable identity. Aud is domesticated mate to Olaf, cooking for him and keeping his house, while seething with love and jealousy:

> ANYA: I am sorry. I simply love you so much...I feel as though I could burst at times...I could not live without you.
> OLAF: Fear not, sweet Aud, you will always be my beautiful girl. ("Selfless," B7.5)

After her lover Olaf betrays her, D'Hoffryn informs Aud that she does not "see her true self" and names her Anyanka:

> ANYA: I am Aud. (pronounced Odd)
> D'HOFFRYN: Are you? Hmm. I'm afraid you don't see your true self. You are Anyanka. I'm a patron of a family of sorts. We're vengeance demons. I'm sure you've heard of us. ("Selfless," B7.5)
> ...
> ANYA: Why do you keep calling me that? My name is Aud.
> D'HOFFRYN: Perhaps, but Anyanka is who you are.

She fights to continually say that her name is Aud, but D'Hoffryn dismisses her comments. D'Hoffryn calls Anyanka her "true self," but it's actually a stereotype. She is one of his many girls, but as he shows by killing Halfrek, they are disposable employees, not cherished family. "I've got plenty of girls. There will always be vengeance demons," he tells her ("Selfless," B7.5). Seeking the purpose he offers, Anyanka goes from happy dark ages housewife to ultra-radical feminist vengeance demon, who murders unfaithful men in cleverly brutal ways. In turn of the century Russia, Anya says, "Vengeance is what I do, Halfrek. I don't need anything else. Vengeance is what I am."

In "The Wish" (B3.9), "Giles names Anyanka when he calls her before him, and moments later, he is the one who destroys that existence. Once again, a male figure has been allowed to create and eliminate an identity for this character. She was selected into vengeance through a male figure and removed from it by another male, not of her own accord" (Francis). Names have power, and here her name is used to rob her of her talisman and purpose (admittedly to save all of Sunnydale).

Stranded in America but still clinging to her old purpose, she says, "I have witnessed a millennium of treachery and oppression from the males of the species and I have nothing but contempt for the whole libidinous lot of them," she says, oblivious to the contradiction as she asks Xander to be her prom date ("The Prom," B3.20).

The name "Anya" is obviously half of Anyanka, as she's been cut in two. She has her demonic memories and experience, but no powers or sense of purpose. Anya is a Russian diminutive of Anna. Thus she's linked with Buffy's middle name, which means grace or divine favor. Perhaps losing her Anyanka identity is meant to be a blessing, if she can only seize hold of it and find her chosen path. Wilcox identifies "Anya" as "a variant of the name for an ordinary girl [Anne] or someone seeking normality" (*Why Buffy Matters* 62). Like Buffy, Anya calls herself Anne/Anya while hiding and pretending to be an ordinary human girl. As Anya, she's terribly lost, as she seduces Xander seeking some sense of belonging, just as she asks him to prom so she can participate in the high school ritual.

Three extra names appear suddenly when she tries defending herself to the Watcher's Council in "Checkpoint," (B5.12), insisting she is pure mainstream American so she won't be exposed as a demon: "Anya Christina Emanuella Jenkins, twenty years old. Born on the fourth of July, and don't think there weren't jokes about that my whole life, mister, 'cause there were. 'Who's our little patriot?' they'd say, when I was younger, and therefore smaller and shorter than I am now." While she determinedly adds three more names to "Anya," along with an American holiday as birthday, they don't give her a sense of purpose. Even the

23

Watcher's Council member dismisses her new identity, only inquiring how to spell "Anya."

Her (invented) middle name Christina simply means she's a Christian, another mainstream label she affixes to herself. Emanuella means "God is with us," a match for Christina and emphasis that she is on the proper side. Her surname, Jenkins, is classic American, with British origins clarifying her upper-class heritage. "Jenkin" originally meant "son of John," a derivation of the most popular of men's names. With mainstream British and religious names, she marks herself as a WASP, the ultimate American insider.

Anya's last name was planned as Emerson in the early seasons, and is thus listed in the yearbook (72). Emerson is another insider name, belonging to the famous transcendentalist writer. He was a champion of individualism, but not perhaps the best choice for Anya, who generally values cash over personal improvement.

Later Anya tries to find an identity through capitalism and the Magic Box, and then agrees to marry Xander. Secretly engaged, she pushes him to reveal their status to the group, once more hoping for a secure public identity: fiancée and wife. Falling into a new stereotype, she sings joyfully of wedding Xander and becoming "his Mrs." in a Disney-style 1950s pink dress with long blonde curls ("Selfless," B7.5).

> (singing) Mr. Xander Harris.
> That's what he is to the world outside.
> That's the name he carries with pride.
> I'm just lately Anya.
> …
> But who am I?
> Now I reply that
> I'm the Missis
> I will be his Missis.
> Mrs. Anya Christina Emanuella Jenkins Harris.
> …
> And I'll be Missis
> I will be his Missis
> Mrs. Anya Lame-Ass-Made-Up-Maiden-Name Harris.

She longs for a name and sense of self like he has. Thus she hopes being his "Mrs." will give her a path in life. However, it would mean trading a new stereotyped persona for all the others she's held. When Xander leaves her at the altar, she strides miserably up the aisle in her white dress, aware that it's meaningless as a sign of identity – she's not going to be a bride. Filled with fury, she takes back the vengeance powers and becomes Anyanka once more. If she is not Xander's, she will be D'Hoffryn's again. "More than any other character, she is anxious about her existence, her mortality, and her role in the world," Mukherjea notes. "What if I'm really nobody?" she asks sadly in "Selfless."

In the same episode, D'Hoffryn and Xander squabble over calling her Anya or Anyanka. D'Hoffryn mentions a "funny historical sidebar" about her original name, but is interrupted when she bursts out, "I wanna take it back." While she apparently means the vengeance spell that killed a room of young men, many scholars note that she seems to want to reclaim *her original name.* She would rather be "odd" and even deserted than an instrument of others' vengeance. "Here, Anya wants to recover the lives of the fraternity members whom she had killed, but this is also a move to reclaim the self. In returning life to the fraternity members, an original name and self may be possible to obtain for Anya, specifically because the desire is her own" (Francis). She tells Xander, "Xander, you can't help me. I'm not even sure there's a me to help." She's making an independent decision without a man guiding her. Anya offers her precious self to accomplish this, but her sister Halfrek is taken in her place. This is a turning point, as Anya realizes, "My whole life, I've just clung to whatever came along," and resolves to find a path for herself without D'Hoffryn or Xander. Anya walks away into the night, more alone than ever.

Aud, lover of Olaf, has been left far far behind in Norway. Though she may have been happier as a lover of rabbits, which she shared freely with her neighbors, that personality was lost long ago. She returns to being Anya, and completes the journey she failed in season three, just after becoming Anya the first time. While she fled Sunnydale before the Mayor's ascension, she stays for the final battle of "Chosen" (B7.22). As she tells Andrew:

> There was this other apocalypse...this one time, and...well, I took off. But this time, I don't...I don't know ... Well, I guess I was kinda new to being around humans before. But now I've seen a lot more, gotten to know people...seen what they're capable of, and I guess I just realized how amazingly screwed-up they all are. I mean really, really screwed-up in a monumental fashion ... And they have no purpose that unites them, so they just drift around, blundering through life until they die...which they...they know is coming, yet every single one of them is surprised when it happens to them. They're incapable of thinking about what they want beyond the moment. They kill each other, which is clearly insane. And yet, here's the thing. When it's something that really matters, they fight. I mean, they're lame morons for fighting, but they do. They never...never quit. So I guess I will keep fighting, too. ("End of Days," B7.21)

To summarize, she wants to be part of the human condition, all of it, including foolish death, in order to save the world. Sadly, she only finds a noble purpose shortly before her sacrifice.

The name Anya may have correspondences with Áine, an Irish goddess of love, summer, and sovereignty. After her husband was cruel to her, she took her revenge by changing him into a goose, killing him, or both. In folklore, Áine is about as close as it gets to a vengeance demon. As a name, Anya is a Russian spin on Anna, and it's definitely increased in use since Joss added her to his cast.

It also must be remarked that Anya is quite close to Buffy's middle name, Anne.

> Like Cordelia, Anya is an occasional Shadow for Buffy. After their similar romances in "The Harsh Light of Day," both are crushed by the male's lack of interest. But while Buffy must live with her mistake, Anya persuades Xander to begin a loving relationship. Much later, Riley's leaving

Buffy pushes Xander into the opposite reaction, and he tells Anya he's in love with her. While Buffy has demon strength, Anya has the inverse – demon memories and arcane knowledge. As their stories progress, they share a forbidden lover in Spike as both try to lose their pain in covert, loveless sex. When Anya expresses Buffy's annoyance with the world, her Faith-like desire to have tantrums and break rules, she is once again the neglected rage, fear, and whim-driven selfishness within Buffy, fighting to be heard. Though she's shallow, Anya is a force for seizing the pleasures of life beside the increasingly-dark and duty-driven Buffy. As Buffy drifts unhappily through season six, Anya's happy engagement and lust for work are her inverted mirror. And like Faith, when Anya goes too far and kills humans, Buffy must rein her in.

In "Selfless" (7.5), as Buffy struggles to allow the repentant sinners Willow and Spike back into her life, Anya expresses the fury Buffy cannot, diving so deep into her former vengeance demon self that she kills an entire house of frat boys. Buffy decides this destructive part of the Scoobies has gone too far. They fight, both in slim black and equally matched. As with Faith, Buffy stabs Anya, pinning her to the wall but not killing her. With Anya trapped there, Buffy can force her to rethink her actions. Anya's boss D'Hoffryn tells her, "You're a big girl, Anyanka. You understand how this works. The proverbial scales must balance. In order to restore the lives of the victims, the fates require a sacrifice" ("Selfless," 7.5). For Anya this is "the life and soul of a Vengeance Demon." For Buffy, this is the rage she's felt. She and Dawn can take their lives back if she lets go of her anger. Anya ends the episode alone, learning that, like Buffy, she must discard all her old identities to discover who she is beneath them all. (Frankel, *Buffy* 116)

Buffy Anne Summers

Buffy (a yuppie eighties name) sounds like a cross between Bunny and Fluffy – the most innocuous helpless damsel most likely to get axed in a horror movie. "In common cultural currency, Buffy suggests an upper-middle-class girl who has few material problems in life. The dissonance in its joining with the term 'the Vampire Slayer' makes for humor of course; but it is also a witty defiance of

27

stereotype" (Wilcox, *Why Buffy Matters* 63). This was a deliberate gesture on Joss Whedon's part: As he put it:

> The first thing I ever thought of when I thought of "Buffy: The Movie" was the little blonde girl who goes into a dark alley and gets killed, in every horror movie. The idea of "Buffy" was to subvert that idea, that image, and create someone who was a hero where she had always been a victim. That element of surprise, genre-busting is very much at the heart of both the movie and the series. (Commentary, "Welcome to the Hellmouth")

The new WB network wanted to name the show "Slayer," but Whedon protested – the jarring mash-up of silly name and serious calling, he felt, was necessary to the franchise.

In "Buffy as Femme Fatale," critic Jason Middleton describes Whedon inventing Buffy as the "beautiful blonde" cheerleader with a name that "could not possibly be coded as more feminine" (161). She triumphs, despite the traditional fate of gorgeous feminine blondes who have sex in horror. As such, she's Whedon's genre-breaker, a rewriting of all the horror tropes.

Buffy is technically short for Elizabeth, linking her with England's most powerful ruling queens who took over the country in times of patriarchy and stunned the world with their strength. Elizabeth means "Pledged to God," and Buffy is indeed the Chosen One, battling forces of evil with a cross shining on her chest. It must be noted, however, that Buffy is *never* called Elizabeth, even on her gravestone – she is "sweet, brave Buffy" only.

In college, she has trouble finding this self:

> XANDER: The point is, you're Buffy.
> BUFFY: Yeah, maybe in high school I was Buffy.
> XANDER: And now in college you're Betty Louise?
> BUFFY: Yeah, I'm Betty Louise Plotnick of East Cupcake, Illinois. Or I might as well be. ("The Freshman," B4.1)

Like her middle name Anne, Betty Louise smacks of countrified normality, rather than the striking name Buffy (which has now come to represent iconic girl power, thanks to the show).

She names herself several times in the series, always a sign of self-determination. In "Anne" (B3.1), for instance, she must call herself "no one" until she bursts out "I'm Buffy the Vampire Slayer. And you are?" Her self-aware quips likewise establish her power over her enemies. In "The Gift" (B5.22) significantly, she meets a vampire who's never heard of her, and she reencounters her roots before her final challenge.

> BUFFY: Wow. Been a long while since I met one who didn't know me.
> ...
> KID: But you're...you're just a girl.
> Buffy pauses in the doorway.
> BUFFY: That's what I keep saying.

No matter how much others label her "just a girl," she's still the slayer.

On Whedonesque.com, libradude pointed out a link between the heroine's name and the "buffy coat" – the thin divider layer in a blood sample after centrifuge that contains most of the white blood cells and platelets. While there's no evidence Whedon made the connection, the fact that "buffy" is the gleaming white layer separating the clear plasma from the red blood cells – like a protective barrier or dividing line between the unseen vampires and blood-filled humans – is delightfully serendipitous.

Meanwhile, Buffy *Summers* and her sister Dawn fight against creatures of the night. The surname suggests sunlight incarnate, enemy of vampires everywhere. Her name also marks her as the destined protector of *Sunny*dale. "Summers" are the mildest, gentlest season, suggestive of vacation. Thus it is a soft, harmless name like "Buffy." It also, as Wilcox notes, suggests a Persephone figure, dying in winter and returning to life in the summer (*Why Buffy Matters* 63). She is the goddess of new life, resurrecting even after she's stolen by death.

The middle name Anne is also worthy of mention. It's a prosaic name, used to emphasize a difference between Buffy's nondescript alias and Chanterelle the exotic mushroom in "Anne" (B3.1):

> LILY: So how come you came up with Anne?
> BUFFY: It's my middle name.
> LILY: Lily's from a song. Rickie picked it. I'm always changing anyway. Chanterelle was part of my exotic phase.
> BUFFY: It's nice. It's a…it's a mushroom.
> LILY: It is? That's really embarrassing.
> BUFFY: Um, well, i-it's an exotic mushroom, if that's any comfort.
> LILY: Well, before that, I was following this loser preacher and calling myself "Sister Sunshine."
> BUFFY: What do they call you at home?
> Lily looks away and doesn't respond.
> BUFFY: I like Lily.

Their conversation reveals much: Lily has completely rejected her past identity and allows men to name her. However by identifying Buffy and reminding her of her heroic past, she's begun to guide Buffy back toward herself. Buffy of course named herself with part of her own name, contrasted with Lily's secrecy and constant switching, all to please her string of boyfriends. By episode's end, the girl has named herself the stronger Anne, after Buffy. She appears several times on *Angel*, as a force for good running a teen center in the worst part of L.A., keeping Buffy's mission and name alive.

Anne also hearkens back, among other things, to the beloved children's series that represents an early offering of girl power: *Anne of Green Gables.* Xander subtly references the series when he says, on Buffy's return from being Anne in L.A., "So skip the heartwarming stuff about kindly old people and saving the farm and get right to the dirt" (This is the plot of Lucy Maud Montgomery's novel *Anne of Green Gables*) in "Dead Man's Party" (B3.2). It must also be mentioned that Kitty Pryde's middle name is Anne. Whedon based much of Buffy's bright, perky personality on the *X-Men* superheroine of his childhood, and the name may be a deliberate homage.

"Anne" means grace or favor. In Christian theology, grace is the spontaneous gift of love and mercy given to people by God through his compassion and generosity, not because humanity has earned it. Buffy receives this divine favor when her frivolous socialite self suddenly receives Slayer powers, which transform her into a superhero. Her previous life was one of selfishness and indulgence, but she is given a gift to transform the world, together with strength and self-defense, though she's clearly done nothing to earn them (in contrast with poor Kendra's lifetime training and deprivation). Another moment of pure grace occurs as snow saves Angel's life in "Amends" (B3.10), just as Buffy's pleading for him to live. Other miracles (though only achieved with her friends' aid) include her return from death twice and Angel's restoration in "Becoming" (B2.22) moments before his death. Buffy has numerous close calls from a near-death at Luke's hands in the series premiere to a photo-finish escape in "Chosen" (B7.22). There are many lucky chances, fortunate coincidences, and other moments when the powers above seem to be protecting her. Angel's protection of her can also be viewed as a type of grace, as she has an "angel" looking after her.

Buffy's other alias is Joan, appearing in "Tabula Rasa" (B6.8). Dawn offers to help, but Buffy names herself, a symbol of strength and determination.

> DAWN: (to Buffy) So you don't have a name?
> BUFFY: Of course I do. I just don't happen to know it.
> DAWN: (smiling) You want me to name you?
> BUFFY: Oh, that's sweet, but I think I can name myself. (thinks) I'll name me...Joan.
> DAWN: (makes a face) Ugh!
> BUFFY: What? Did you just 'ugh' my name?
> DAWN: No! I just...I mean, it's so blah. Joan?
> BUFFY: I like it. I feel like a Joan.

Joan is a variant of John, the most common name. It's also

the original name of Lily, according to "Lie to Me's" shooting script, and thus the name of someone who hides from danger and needs rescuing. Possibly the chosen one is eager to get a "blah" name and retire from being a hero, but in fact, in this episode, she's more Buffylike than in the rest of her miserable sixth season. Having so-named herself, she instantly takes charge and battles the vampires. Thus Joan doesn't seem like an ordinary identity after all, but a heroic one – Joan of Arc. "When Buffy chooses her name, she chooses the name of a woman warrior who dies for her cause" (Wilcox, *Why Buffy Matters* 61). Even without her identity, she still chooses to be Buffy.

Daniel "Oz" Osbourne
Whedon notes: "I just knew a guy named Oz. Kinda short. Played lead guitar for a band. He had this incredible cool about him; he wore bowling shirts before anyone else did" (Havens 62).

His real name is only mentioned after he leaves Sunnydale in "Wild at Heart" (B4.6). As such, he's better known as Oz, linked with a bad boy image from the prison TV show, as well as with the fantasy world of Baum, all in a single laconic syllable. It should also be noted that Oz is a nickname for Australia, home of the "Dingoes ate my baby" tale that inspired his band.

The name Daniel means "God is my judge," not the most appropriate identity for one who plays God for Halloween. (Notably, no one ever calls him Daniel – he seems to agree.) The more intriguing last name, Osbourne, comes from the Viking word for bear-god, the berserker who turns into a bear. Aside from the choice of animal, this is a nearly perfect fit. The medieval English surname lingered after the Viking invasions, linking the two cultures, gentlemen and savages, in the person of Oz.

Dawn Summers
"Dawn [as in the sunrise] is forever young, never aging, never dying, she follows her destiny and sees generation

succeed generation," as Jean Chevalier and Alain Gheerbrant explain in *A Dictionary of Symbols* (275). Thus dawn is a symbol of total potentiality and hope for the future. In Judeo-Christian lore, Dawn symbolizes God's victory over the world of darkness, the golden light that appears at the end of "Chosen" (B7.22). Dawn represents the sunlight and new world that Buffy fights and dies to create.

Welsh literature commonly describes dawn as "the youth of the day" (Chevalier and Gheerbrant 275). She's both the most youthful character on the show and literally only a few months old – symbolically the most vulnerable. Whedon comments:

> I wanted somebody who wasn't at the exact same stage in life that all my other characters were. Who was younger, so we got a different perspective on everything they do and also somebody who happens to have a different relationship with Buffy we've never seen her have before. Which is sort of a squabbling sister, pretentious yet a very charged relationship that we haven't seen in her life [...] She's fourteen and it's good to have somebody who's still about to go through what they went through. ("Joss Whedon at Wizard World")

Faith Lehane

Faith is a name straight from Puritan values along with Hope, Charity, Prudence, and all the rest. It, unlike some of Whedon's favorites, was always a common women's name. "Faith had been on the rise for a decade when Joss used the name, and would peak a few years after the character slayed her first vamp" (appellationmountain).

It's a jarring choice for this thoroughly modern girl who has faith in no one at all – she rejects individual offers of help and friendship from Giles, Angel, Xander, Wesley, Willow, and especially Buffy over and over. Writer Doug Petrie describes the character's name as "wildly ironic" due to her cynical nature. According to Petrie, "She's the most faithless character we've got. She doesn't trust herself or anyone around her. We try to do that a lot with our monsters. It's much more fun if you look at it from their point of view" (Golden, Bissette and Sniegoski).

After she flees to the show *Angel,* however, she transforms. Angel shows perfect faith in her in "Sanctuary" (A1.19) as he offers his life to protect her. He takes her side against his precious Buffy, then proves willing for the police to lock him in a sunny cell and kill him – all to defend the murderess who beat up his team.

Faith responds to this gesture as she never responded to the characters on *Buffy*: She turns herself in and patiently submits to jail. Only when Angelus returns does she break out, telling Wesley that Angel is the only person never to give up on her. In season eight, she plays a similar role. Faith undertakes Angel's rehabilitation and redemption as he did for her in "Sanctuary." This proves to be a long road.

Through the *Angel and Faith* comic book arc, she cares for the distraught, maddened vampire, protecting him on his (apparently) insane quest to collect scattered fragments of Giles's soul. By the end, Faith has grown weary of the disheartening quest and decides to work with Kennedy in private security. However, she takes solace in the knowledge that she's restored Angel to sanity through her faith in him. Unfortunately, Giles (who had mentored her during season eight) tells her Buffy is his priority, and she leaves him, hurt and abandoned once again.

Whedon created the surname "Lehane," for her in January 2005, during the creation of Eden Studios' *Buffy the Vampire Slayer* role-playing game. Whedon explained at the time: "There was this role playing game or something. They said she hadda have a last name for her so I chose Lehane 'cause I wanted something Southie" (Whedonesque.com).

Lehane is in fact Irish, from the Gaelic "O'Liathain," meaning "descendant of Liathan." "Liath" means grey, and Faith is a terribly grey character, as she proves with the expedient morality in season three.

BUFFY: We help people! It doesn't mean we can do whatever we want.
FAITH: Why not? … You're still not seeing the big picture, B. Something made us different. We're warriors. We're built to kill.
BUFFY: To kill demons! But it does not mean that we get to pass judgment on people like we're better than everybody else!
FAITH: We are better! That's right, better. People need us to survive. In the balance, nobody's gonna cry over some random bystander who got caught in the crossfire.
BUFFY: I am.
FAITH: Well, that's your loss. ("Consequences," B3.15).

In the comic *No Future for You* (B8.2), she uses the alias Hope Lyonne. Hope is obviously a play on Faith, Hope and Charity, while Lyonne is a French place name, both a play on Lehane and an upgrade to the British peerage for her role. It also (less than coincidentally) emphasizes she's fierce as a lion.

Riley Finn
Fionn mac Cumhaill was an Irish culture hero, a great supernatural warrior augmented with magical strength. He accomplished great feats, but his beautiful bride finally ran off with another man.

Riley means valiant and Finn means white or fair-haired. In everything he does, he's certainly brave, proper, and noble. His name is very Irish (both names), indicating his family origins though he's from middle America. As such, he represents classic American values – belief in the military and male hierarchy – that come into conflict with modern outspoken women. He's also very conservative, as he attends church and joins the Initiative. As Spike points out, he's not nearly bad-boy enough for Buffy: "What've you got? A piercing glance? Face it, white bread, Buffy's got a type and you're not it. She likes us dangerous, rough, occasionally bumpy in the forehead region. Not that she doesn't like you, but, sorry, Charlie – You're just not dark enough" ("Shadow," B5.8). Unfortunately for Riley, this is true.

Rupert "Ripper" Giles

Giles means "young goat" in Greek. Goats were associated with Paganism during the Christian era, marking Giles as a member of Buffy's magical Wiccan community, rather than the mainstream culture. The Semitic god-god Azazel became demonized as a scapegoat (giving us the modern word), much as Giles is scapegoated by the Watcher's Council and sometimes Buffy's mother from the crimes of the rebellious slayer.

"The fact that he has two 'first' names (Rupert Giles) allows him to be regularly called 'Giles' by the teen characters without this ever sounding strange (as it might if they called him 'Smith') and suggesting a degree of intimacy while not quite putting them on the same footing," Lorna Jowett notes in her book on gender, *Sex and the Slayer* (127).

Rupert, a German variant of Robert, means "Bright Fame." Of course, it's a bit more exotic to American ears than Robert, setting Giles apart from the American mainstream.

Giles' teenage nickname "Ripper" is presumably from Jack the Ripper. (Though the Angel and Faith comic *Daddy Issues* suggests an alternative similar to the origins of "William the Bloody Awful Poet": As a boy Giles constantly played with a toy airplane. After he tore his aunt's minidress, she said they should have called the little blighter Ripper.

The Ripper persona is the complete opposite of Giles. He represents Giles's aggression, bursting out in the four Ethan Rayne episodes complete with working class accent (actually the actor's own). Giles's Ripper costuming in "Band Candy" (B3.6) "associates him with either a working-class hero (like early Marlon Brando) or, perhaps, a middle-class would-be rebel like James Dean in *Rebel Without a Cause*" (Jowett 130). Though he attempts to be the tweed-wearing librarian who only helps behind the scenes, he brings a Ripper-like ferocity and expediency to the team when needed.

Spike/William Pratt

William means "resolute protection" as Spike once was for his mother, and becomes for Buffy and Dawn, especially in "The Gift" (B5.22) and "Chosen" (B7.22). In his youngest appearance, he's a shy, beauty-seeking Victorian who writes poetry and longs hopelessly for Cecily. "'Fool for Love' (B5.7) shows the 'good man' he once was and perhaps could be again, the one who politely courts a young woman and cares for his mother. But we don't see him revert to this poetry-reading, self-accepting man until the final episode of *Angel*" (Frankel, *Buffy* 138).

When he was called William, Cecily spurned him, his mother rejected him, and Angel taunted his weakness. His last name, Pratt, suggests that he is in fact a bit of a Pratt, as useless and proper as Wesley before his character growth. "It would be a little embarrassing for a die-hard killer to admit that in his past incarnation he was practically scared of his own shadow, and accordingly vampire Spike attempts to downplay his 'William side' as much as possible, in favour of being known as the much more impressive double Slayer-slayer" (Lowe). He becomes William the Bloody – ironic, since this is actually related to his poetry:

> ARISTOCRAT 1: Have you heard? They call him William the Bloody because of his bloody awful poetry!
> ARISTOCRAT 2: It suits him. I'd rather have a railroad spike through my head than listen to that awful stuff!
> ("Fool for Love," B5.7)

Thus Spike creates a new identity for himself: Slayer of slayers, most fearsome of all. "Spike is the name of his own choosing: it is phallic, it is violent, and it is clearly embedded in response to the mockery of the shy young poet" (Wilcox, *Why Buffy Matters* 59). He affects a lower-class accent and wears rougher clothes before finding his iconic leather jacket in the seventies.

> Of course Spike, our vampire-du-jour, sees himself as a pretty cool monster: a ruthless, bloody killer who got his

nickname by torturing his victims with railroad spikes. He is over one hundred years old, and in a century or more of vampiredom he has left a lot of carnage in his wake, including (as he is proud to relate) the bodies of two previous Slayers. (Lowe)

Upon his first appearance in "School Hard," (B2.3), Spike shrouds his identity in mystery:

> SPIKE: Nice work, baby.
> BUFFY: Who are you?
> SPIKE: You'll find out on Saturday.
> BUFFY: What happens on Saturday?
> SPIKE: I kill you.
>
> SHEILA: Who are you?
> SPIKE: Who do you want me to be?

When asked if Angel knows his name, Angel likewise identifies him as terrifying, noting, "Once he starts something he doesn't stop, until everything in his path is dead. Stay away."

When Spike is introduced, he is intended merely as an impulsive, villainous "Big Bad," taunting Buffy and Angel but losing the big conflicts. Though he maintains his love for Drusilla which "stinks of humanity," all other human characteristics have been banished. Still, the William personality still exists below the surface, desperate for love and starved for sunlight.

His human "will" grows through the series, cultivated as he cultivates morality and a soul. Buffy calls him William at significantly human moments, pulling back from his sincere feelings in "Fool for Love" and acknowledging his soul in season seven. "Notably, in her rejection, she calls him William, a name that invokes his human (and feminized) side" (Jowett 161). In Spike's final episode on *Angel*, he reads from the poetry he wrote as William so long ago, exposing the most vulnerable human self that was mocked and taunted out of existence.

Nonetheless, he does not resume the name William,

instead reclaiming his leather coat, cigarettes, and bad boy attitude in "Get it Done" (B7.15), when Buffy insists he fight at full strength. In "Tabula Rasa" (B6.8) he confuses his name with Buffy's stakes – he is "Buffy's weapon of choice" (Wilcox, *Why Buffy Matters* 61). He turns from being her enemy to her "resolute protector" and slowly regains his William qualities as he regains his soul. Nonetheless, he's still Spike.

Tara Maclay

Tara, means earth, suggesting comfort, feminine magic, and generosity of spirit. She dresses in earth tones and tells Dawn to eat her vegetables, an earth mother and nurturing goddess in every way. "Tara" often refers to Ireland, home of earth magic, fairy magic, and the evanescent spirit that fades as quickly as Tara herself. Her last name, also Irish, comes from clay – earth yet again. "Of course, Willow, the tree, is rooted in Tara, the earth – and uprooted when Tara is lost," Wilcox notes (*Why Buffy Matters* 50). She is not only the wiccan earth magic but Willow's constant foundation.

Tārā is the name of a set of bodhisattvas, or Buddhist deities. Just as Tara Maclay is the Scoobies' "mom," Tārā is the force of the feminine principle. Known as the Mother of Mercy and Compassion, she gives birth to kindness, empathy and relief from bad karma as she loves all the people under her protection.

Each "color" of Tārā represents a different aspect or virtue: White Tārā brings maternal compassion, healing, and serenity. Red Tārā teaches how to discriminate and how to turn raw desire into compassion and love. Blue Tārā is a protector who defends the innocent with a ferocious female energy and engenders swift spiritual awakening. Green Tārā, the Buddha of enlightened activity, protects her followers from fear.

Of course, when Tara Maclay dies, the Scoobies lose all these qualities – several Scoobies give in to the First's paranoia and despair without Tara to ground them.

Fearing Tara's loss, Willow uses magic to keep her, trying to create love artificially rather than honestly. When Tara leaves Willow, she loses her judgment and becomes addicted to magic. Without the righteous anger and protective fury of Blue Tara, Willow unleashes her rage indiscriminately, determined to destroy the innocent like Dawn as well as the guilty. Willow is filled with wrath and only Xander's love (in a weaker substitution for Tara's) saves her from destroying the earth.

Willow Danielle Rosenberg

A willow tree is commonly regarded as graceful and feminine. It grows near water (another feminine symbol) and is often associated with magic and particularly Wiccans. "Some believe that the word 'wicca,' used for the European tradition of witchcraft, came from the word 'wicker,' meaning willow" (Shepherd 242). Willow wood is known to repel evil spirits (Watts 137). At the same time, the willow grows rapidly and has deep tough roots, suggesting the character's hidden strength. The willow is a tree of inspiration, intuition, and dream, establishing the character as a font of concealed wisdom in research as well as magic.

Willows were magical – it was said one could kill at a distance by tying knots in supple willow branches (Watts 26). Chinese farmers used willow branches to invoke rain, while the Welsh used them to cure toothache and ague. Willow bark was a primitive aspirin in Europe. Because of their association with water, willows could also be symbols of resurrection (Watts 426). In China, they symbolize immortality. Willow, as shown in the season eight comics, lives many centuries into the future because of her magic.

Willows have for a very long time been symbols of sorrow and of forsaken love (emphasizing Willow's betrayal of Tara in season six as well as their doomed romance) (Watts 425). Weeping willows, as they're known for their trailing branches, were symbols of sorrow, grief, and mourning, again tying into Willow's arc in seasons six and seven. The willow tree was sacred to Osiris, the Egyptian god of death whom Willow summons several times. The Romans considered in a tree of war, naming it *bellicum* after *bellum,* battle (Shepherd 242). In the sixth and seventh seasons, Willow certainly fulfils this role.

Willow is an aphrodisiac in some cultures (Watts 10). While Buffy fails to find a real relationship with Spike in seasons five through eight, Willow provides a contrast with her true love for Tara, then Kennedy.

Buffy walks around surrounded by wills. She has Willow (often called Will), Angel (his original name Liam is a variant on William) and Spike (William the Bloody). For Buffy, all these conflicting energies strengthen her when she falters, as these characters themselves frequently do. Wilcox suggests that having so many Wills suggests a link between good and bad characters and a lack of black and white morality (as discussed in "Lie to Me" when Buffy kills Billy Fordham). Wholly good and wholly bad are an illusion – there are Wills all along the spectrum (*Why Buffy Matters* 52). When Buffy is torn over Angelus in season two, Willow suddenly grows in strength to order everyone about and save Angel for Buffy. In other episodes, such as "Choices" (B3.19) and "Bargaining" (B6.1) Willow's strength brings life to Buffy.

Describing the Final Girl in horror movies, critic Jason Middleton explains, "She is represented as less conventionally sexually attractive; favoring boyish 'practical' clothing; she is not sexually promiscuous; she possess a detective-like curiosity; and she has an ambiguously gendered name such as Stretch, Will, Joey, or Max" (161). As such, the androgynously nicknamed Will fits well, while Buffy is the ultra-feminine girly girl who nonetheless trounces the monsters in Whedon's subversion. Her masculine nickname is tough, while also emphasizing her role as sidekick rather than main focus.

"If there's a Whedon success story when it comes to names, Willow would be the star. The TV show debuted in 1997 and Willow entered the chart for the first time at

#853. She is now at her highest at #171" (appellationmountain). "The name has transcended its one-time hippie aura to move into the realm of reappraised and appreciated nature names...Willow is even more popular in other English-speaking countries: it's Number 43 in Australia and in the Top 100 in the UK, Canada and Scotland" (Satran and Rosenkrantz).

Willow struggles with identity in the series as her many roles all shift about: sidekick, researcher, perfect student, substitute teacher and tutor, assistant slayer, Jew, lesbian, wiccan, witch. Most of these are temporary and not strongly held. "This extravagant range of interests and roles is evidence of the fact that there appears to be no core identity to Willow – nothing that defines her" (South 134). As she worries that she lacks Tara's lesbian and Wiccan experience or tries to highlight her importance to the group, it's Tara who reassures her over and over. Thus Willow is shattered on Tara's death and redefines herself as a seething font of rage and vengeance.

> WILLOW: (scoffs) Let me tell you something about Willow. She's a loser. And she always has been. People picked on Willow in junior high school, high school, up until college. With her stupid mousy ways. And now? Willow's a junkie.
> BUFFY: I can help.
> WILLOW: The only thing Willow was ever good for...
> She pauses, drops the bitter sarcasm and grows pensive.
> WILLOW: ...the only thing I had going for me...were the moments – just moments – when Tara would look at me and I was wonderful. (grimly) And that will never happen again. ("Two to Go," B2.21)

Of course, Xander manages to stop her with his love, and more, his reminder of how he sees her – who she always has been. In the next episode, after time in England, she's reformed and found herself again:

> GILES: Do you want to be punished?
> WILLOW: I wanna be Willow.
> GILES: You are. In the end, we all are who we are, no

matter how much we may appear to have changed. ("Lessons," B7.1).

> At the beginning of season seven, Giles has gone "all Dumbledore" and taken Willow to England for healing. She's gone from suppressed, lobotomized instincts to raging, out-of-control emotion and learned that neither is the right path. The best recourse is to seek guidance and relearn the deep feminine instincts. This Willow does with a coven in England who teaches her gentle, healing magic she can release bit by bit, indulging her creative side without cutting it off to fester in the dark. She embraces earth magic of "the root systems, the molecules, the energy," learning how everything's connected and how to care for her own mishandled magic ("Lessons," B7.1). Once she rooted herself in Tara MaClay (two names that mean earth). Now she draws her power from the real earth, a more everlasting foundation. (Frankel, *Buffy* 175)

She reclaims her name, no longer calling herself the "vengeance" or "the magic." Once more restored to understanding and goodness, Willow finds a similar relationship in her next girlfriend, Kennedy, who offers to be the string to Willow's kite.

Willow's middle name was given in an early draft of "Bad Girls" (B3.14). Danielle means "God is my judge" and links her with Oz, whose real name is Daniel. As Willow's morality slips, especially in season six, she's equated to an addict who must finally "let go and let God" – accept the interconnectedness of the world and her personal responsibility therein.

Rosenberg is a Germanic last name meaning "mountain of roses" or red mountain. Thus Willow is associated with the rose as well as the willow tree. "Throughout the classical world and in the near east, roses were synonymous with beauty, fertility, and purity" (Shepherd 261). In alchemy, the rose symbolizes the blossoming of the spirit, as Willow, the gentle "Spiritus" of the show, grows in power. Roses were sacred to Aphrodite, goddess of love, but also to the Muses, demigoddesses of creative force, and Dionysus, god of reckless abandon, all influences of Willow's personality.

Of course, like Willow, roses also have a darker side. The flowers have a mythic connection with blood, mostly because of their deep red color. In the Christian tradition, red roses are associated with the grail that caught the blood of Jesus, while an ancient poem states, "On battlefields where a number of heroes have been slain, roses or eglantines will grow" (Chevalier and Gheerbrant 813-814). Many myths see red roses or anemones blossoming from the blood of a dying god. They traditionally appeared at funerals and on tombs, marking them as a flower of death like the lily (Watts 103). The image of Willow's "red mountain" suggests a pile of the dead, after she turns evil in season six and is shown becoming dark Willow again in the dystopian future of season eight.

Angel Investigations

Angel/Angelus/Liam

In the pilot he introduces himself as "Angel," for he considers himself Buffy's guardian angel, who swore to protect her when she was chosen. His behavior also hints at his future of stalking Buffy (even when he's not evil).

> BUFFY: Uh, we're having this thing at school.
> ANGEL: Career week?
> BUFFY: How did you know?
> ANGEL: I lurk. ("What's My Line," B2.9)

He sneaks around Sunnydale spying on her in "Pangs" (B4.8) and has a one-sided relationship with her in "I Will Remember You" (A1.8) (the evidence suggests he never tells her of it). We also discover he's set spies on her at the end of *Angel* season five.

Though he has a demon inside, he's very much a Christian angel, complete with martyr tendencies. He offers his life for flawed characters like Faith and Darla, as well as his beloved Buffy. In the final episode, Angel quotes

44

Jesus, saying, "This may come out a little pretentious, but one of you will betray me." Spike pertly responds, "Can I deny you three times?" He is pictured as a sacrificed saint several times, with Buffy's cross burned into his chest and his dying to save the world in season two. The Shanshu prophecy emphasizes that he will be a leader in the apocalypse, like the archangels, God's warriors. At the beginning of season five, Angel discovers that Wolfram and Hart tried to turn him into a ghost. Though it's too pat to suggest Angel's name foreshadows his move to Los Angeles, this similarity of names is referenced in the pilot, "City of..." (A1.1)

"The name had a good run while the character was on TV, and remains in the US Top 100 for boys. But this one probably has less to do with Whedon, and more to do with Angel's popularity among Spanish-speaking parents" (appellationmountain).

This name is unfortunately ironic when considering his inner demon. When the demon is freed, he has another name – Angelus – the monster with an Angel's face. This name is the more foreign and old-fashioned version, compared with the approachable American Angel.

Yet Angelus, the repressed shadow, can do everything Angel can't. When he sleeps with Buffy and loses his soul, we see him tormenting her friends who have always despised him. On a smaller scale, Angelus mocks Cordelia's theater performance in "Eternity" (A1.17), whereas Angel feels he must be polite and repress his true feelings. Angelus is everything he can't say, can't express. When he turns cruel, he transmutes his feelings, but still has them – As Willow says to Buffy, "You're still the only thing he thinks about" ("Passion," B2.17).

The two sides are bound together, with the repressed one always howling for acknowledgement. In "Orpheus" (A4.15), Angel and Angelus both see their life flash before their eyes, until Angel can grow strong enough to take their body back and chain up his evil side.

Liam only appears a few times in the series – in

45

"Belonging" (B2.21), he flirts with Darla, a beautiful blonde who offers him a new purpose and mission much as Buffy does. Like Buffy, she tells him to close his eyes and kills him. "The Prodigal" (A1.15) deals with his bad relationship with his father, stealing the silver to go drinking and wenching. It's possible these emotions appear once more when he tortures Giles in "Becoming" (B2.22) or is especially cruel to his vampire "children," Drusilla, Spike, James, Penn, and Lawson, as well as Connor. In "Somnambulist" (A1.11), Penn tells him, "Well, you were right about one thing, Angelus. The last 200 years has been about me sticking it to my father. But I've come to realize something – it's you! You made me! You taught me! You approved of me in ways my mortal father never did! You are my real father, Angelus." In "Spin the Bottle" (B4.6), Angel transforms into Liam (mentally at least), and Connor is shocked at how much they have in common.

> CONNOR: Fathers. Don't they suck?
> ANGEL: Say one thing, then... "Be good. Fear God. Do as you're told." And the whole while I know good and well, he's had his share of sinning.
> CONNOR: Sounds kinda like my father.
> ANGEL: Is he a self-righteous bastard?
> CONNOR: You'd be amazed.

A fourth side of Angel is present in his inner demon, seen in Pylea and in "The Dark Age" (B2.8). While Angel uses it as a tool in the latter, Pylea sees him weeping and howling, deeply ashamed that he hosts a monster inside. Nonetheless, the final episode sees him come to terms with his demon as Spike embraces his buried inner poet.

> HAMILTON: Let me say this as clearly as I can. You cannot beat me. I am a part of them. The Wolf, Ram, and Hart. Their strength flows through my veins. My blood is filled with their ancient power.
> ANGEL: Can you pick out the one word there you probably shouldn't have said?

For the first time in the series, Angel uses his vampire

powers to drain the enemy and absorb his power. He is vampire and finally glories in it.

Angel and Spike

Their names are linked, as Liam is a derivation of William. Likewise, the name Angel is feminized and spiritual, protective and distant, while Spike is phallic and immediate, a physical weapon. This linkage emphasizes that they are mirrors for each other. Each embodies everything the other has rejected in his life.

Jung postulates that one's rejected or unexplored issues fester within as the Shadow – in this way, Buffy gravitates toward Faith and imitates her in "Bad Girls" (B3.14), slipping into her shadow and experimenting with a different lifestyle. One can bring aspects of the personality to the forefront (like Buffy does in "When She Was Bad" or "Anne") or meet someone who embodies these lost qualities and forces a character to face them (like Faith or Lily does). Thus just as Spike and William, Angel and Angelus, and Angelus and Liam are Jungian shadow aspects of the same person, Spike and Angel are shadows for each other as well.

In the fifth season of *Angel*, they're seen exasperating each other in every episode, as they compete on every level: for the role of champion, for the Shanshu prophecy, for status, for Buffy. "Is this really the destiny that was meant for you? Do you even really want it? Or is it that you just want to take something away from me?" Angel demands in "Destiny" (A5.8).

We see Spike and Angel's respective shadows clearly, as becoming a vampire means each can become his own polar opposite and unleash the self he's always repressed. Liam – who always acted on impulse cavorting in bars, stealing from his own hated father, and longing for real adventure – transforms under Darla's bite: Liam, who never takes any responsibility, becomes Angelus, leader of a family. As he scolds Spike for endangering the womenfolk, he's turned into a mirror of his own father in a

47

way, yelling at the younger, reckless, fun-loving vampire who resembles his old human self.

Angelus is the force of adulthood. Further, Angelus spends 150 years with the same woman and perfects cruelty into an art, destroying Drusilla piece by piece because it's "all about finesse" ("Fool for Love," B5.7). Even after he transforms into the soulful Angel, he retains that darkness and exquisite cruelty, as we see him threaten and torture for information on his own show.

Spike was once William the Bloody Awful Poet and complete Mama's boy. He was determined to be a good man and seek beauty in life. However, one bite from Drusilla (who likewise turns from the purest girl in the world to a wanton demonness) changes him forever. Spike (who soon after changes his name) can impale his critics on railroad spikes and become the badass he never was as a polite, repressed human in Victorian society. He wants to destroy, so he does. "As vampires go, Spike is actually very immature, he's very young," Marsters says ("Spike, Me" Featurette). "He's a sociopath who enjoys killing people and ripping their lungs out but at the same time he's a very sensitive guy." And throughout the series, he's desperate to be identified as villainous, evil, scary. Everything, in short, that William could never be. In all his incarnations as ambitious vampire brat, punk rocker, new vampire act in town, and amoral demon slayer, he expresses all his feelings, on the spot. He abandons plans and seems determined to only "have a bit of fun." The most repressed human has become the most heedless of characters.

Connor /Steven Franklin Thomas Holtz/Connor Reilly
"Connor" is derived from the Gaelic name "Coachuhhar," meaning "high desire or strong will." As Connor repeatedly defies Angel, he certainly demonstrates that. His name may be a subtle nod to the *Roseanne* family, the Conners – one of Whedon's earliest writing jobs. Of course, he was played by babies Connor, Jake, and Trenton Tupen, so it's likely the writers thought the actual baby's name would fit well.

Connor was a semi-legendary king of Ulster in Irish epic. He was supposed to rule for only a year, but in that year he won the people's loyalty, just as Angel's son slowly takes over Angel Investigations in the comics. His name means "lover of hounds." Connor is an expert tracker, and in fact, a pack of demon dogs are devoted to him in the *Angel and Faith* comics. In the story, he's a strong king, but not the true hero – in fact, Connor makes bad choices and the supernatural Cu Chulain, his foster son, must save him. Angel and Connor have this relationship, with father and son roles reversed.

Steven (the name Connor was given by Holtz) is an English name and variant of the Greek Stephen meaning "crowned one." He's certainly Holtz's appointed heir, though replacing an Irish name with an English one appears to be the central point. Holtz gives him the middle names "Franklin Thomas" in "Sleep Tight" (A3.16), but it's not clear who his namesakes are. All are names of the British establishment, as Holtz tries to mold Connor into his son rather than Angel's.

Angel bargains for a spell to remake Connor's life at the end of season four, and Connor becomes the son of Laurence and Colleen Reilly. This is an Irish last name, matching well with Connor's Irish first name. It also links him with Riley Finn, another warrior for good who must make hard choices about which side to take. Riley means "courageous," a quality Connor certainly possesses, though now he can become a well-grounded hero without the rage and confusion that define him as Angel's son. In the comics, with both sets of memories, Connor matures and tells Angel that the spell gave him the stability he needed.

Charles Gunn

The last name suggests violence (though as he points out, it's his proper last name, with two n's). The first name is the classic Charles, rather than Charlie or Chuck. Even on the street, without a high school degree, he maintains a certain propriety in how he refers to himself.

> Charles is a longtime traditional favorite that was in the Top 10 until the 1960s. Lately Charles has been resuscitated by many celeb parents, from Jodie Foster to Russell Crowe, honoring a distinguished history dating back to the emperor Charlemagne – the original Charles the Great. Charles has been so well used for so long that it is virtually faceless – it can conjure up anyone from Dickens to Chaplin to Bronson. It has been an elegant royal name – designating both Bonnie Prince Charlie, leader of a 1745 rebellion, and the present Prince of Wales, as well as kings of France, Spain, England, Portugal and Hungary. (Satran and Rosenkrantz)

"Charles" from the French means "free man," an appropriate name considering how he lives before joining Angel Investigations. Besides his sister, he has no responsibilities or encumbrances. He leads a loosely-knit gang, fights vampires, and does as he wishes. He's even sold his soul, freeing him from that burden as well.

Of course, he has the fastest character transformation of all, with a single brain adjustment recreating him as Charles Gunn, Esquire. Intriguingly, he barely changes his name (unlike Spike/William, Angel/Angelus, Fred/Illyria, or Lorne/Krevlorneswath). And those at Wolfram and Hart comment on his potential. Perhaps this is who he, as Charles Gunn, has always been meant to be, if he'd had the opportunity. Once a lawyer for Wolfram and Hart, he actually inherits Cordelia's role on the team – she was the link to the Powers that Be, and he is the conduit to the Senior Partners in the White Room.

In his new role, he has far more responsibility – he is no longer leader of a street gang but an enormous corporation with supernatural and physical powers. He discovers how much he values his new self when he feels his special skill fading. He returns to the doctor, who offers to fix him in return for a favor with customs. Unfortunately, Fred's life is the ultimate price for this act.

In response, the cultured lawyer vanishes, replaced by the tough Gunn who's all man. The final episode sees him helping Anne back in his old neighborhood and fighting to the death, embracing his origins even with his new powers of law.

In *Angel: After the Fall*, he's transformed into a vampire and must face his monstrous side along with his hatred for Angel. Eventually, the senior partners erase this storyline, but the memories linger, of all Gunn did. He does not change names before or after, emphasizing that this savagery also dwells within him.

Cordelia Chase

Cordelia, often a mild antagonist on *Buffy*, is confidence personified. While Buffy is an outsider at her school, the oddly behaving girl who cannot make Homecoming Queen, Cordelia has everything, from "the Cordettes" and clothes down to the "Queen C" car. Her last name, Chase, suggests activity but mostly her popularity – she is the one the boys pursue. It's also alliterative, like many superhero names.

Her name hints at *Anne of Green Gables*. This early girl-power novel features the main character Anne who hates how plain and unglamorous she is, like Buffy who shares a name with her. Anne says in the first book, "I would love to be called Cordelia. It's such a perfectly elegant name," and she keeps up the fantasy, requesting that people call her that. Buffy similarly wishes she could be Cordelia, the elegant popular girl who can date and dress well without being interrupted by vampire slaying.

She also offers the uncomfortable truths other characters don't wish to acknowledge. Her most famous namesake, from Shakespeare's *King Lear,* was banished from her father's court because she couldn't dissimulate. "The tart-tongued cheerleader is one of the series' major truth-tellers" (Wilcox, *Why Buffy Matters* 47). As we discover in "Earshot" (B3.18), she always says exactly what she's thinking.

She continues to set the characters straight on *Angel*, cutting through their politeness. "So you two are groin buddies?" she asks Angel and Eve. "And I thought Darla was rock bottom" ("You're Welcome," A5.12). Her visions are another reflection of her truth telling, as they show what is really happening in the world, and Cordelia blurts them to her friends. She has become an oracle – one whose words always come true, though sometimes in an unexpected way.

On *Angel*, she's the spiritual inspiration of the team as she literally connects with the Powers that Be and brings their messages to Angel, and reminds him of his mission to help the hopeless. In "Fredless" (A3.5), Fred names Wesley as "the brain," Gun as "the muscle," and Cordy as "the heart." The root of Cordelia, related to "cardio" in fact means "heart."

Season four, her pregnancy sees her growing duplicitous – our cue that she's no longer in control. However, comatose, her blood offers a serum that lets people see Jasmine as she truly is. Even unconscious, she is a conduit to truth.

In her final appearance, she makes it her mission to tell Angel the hard truths. He is working for the devil, seduced with fast cars and fancy toys. "Don't give me that, 'everything's fine here' company line. I'm not buying it. Neither are you. And neither are the Powers That Be. Why do you think they woke me up, gave me that vision? They know you slipped the track, and they want me to help put you back on it" ("You're Welcome," A5.12). Just before she vanishes, her final act is to share her visions with Angel, showing him how to bring down the forces of evil. In the comics she appears again, as guide and protector, and especially as Angel's heart.

Lorne/Krevlorneswath of the Deathwok Clan

> Landok: Can it really be you? Krevlorneswath of the Deathwok Clan?
> LORNE: It's clearly rabid. Do your thing, Angel.
> ANGEL: Krevlorneswath?
> CORDY: Of the Deathwok Clan?
> LORNE: I prefer Lorne.
> ANGEL: Lorne?

LORNE: Yes. Lorne, if you must. Though I generally
don't go by that because... green.
CORDY: Huh?
ANGEL: Right! Lorne Greene!
[Cordelia and Wesley look puzzled]
ANGEL: *Bonanza!*
[Cordelia and Wesley still look puzzled]
ANGEL: Fifteen years on the air not mean anything to
anyone here?
[Cordelia and Wesley continue to look puzzled]
ANGEL: Okay, now I feel old. ("Belonging," A2.19)

Krevlorneswath of the Deathwok Clan rejects his entire identity when he finds himself in L.A. From a world of warriors, he builds a place of total peace, the demon sanctuary Caritas. As he tells Angel and his team later, "All my life I thought I was crazy. That I had ghosts in my head or something. Simply because I could hear music. Of course I didn't know it was music. All I knew was that it was something beautiful and – and painful – and right. And I was the only one who could hear it. – Then I wound up here and heard Aretha for the first time..." ("Over the Rainbow," A2.20). His new name is as theatrical and Hollywood-centric as he is. He reinvents himself as a nightclub owner surrounded by music, and he does his best to avoid returning to Pylea.

His nickname of the "Host" is not just a way to avoid being called the silly "Lorne Green." He's distancing himself from his old name as well, and hiding behind his job: nightclub host and aid to lost souls. However, in Pylea, he must retake his former identity. As he notes, "To the people of Pylea a host is just one more thing to lay your eggs in" ("Through the Looking Glass," A2.21). By the later seasons, everyone calls him Lorne and he's moved out of the Nightclub to be a member of Angel's team. He's growing, though like Spike and Angel, he can never take back his past.

Wesley Wyndam-Pryce
Wesley is an English name, meaning "western meadow."

Meadows often represent freedom and openness, or a gentle place of fertile imagination. However, considering his original appearance in Buffy season three, Wesley must be considered for its association with propriety and England. It's also possible the name was created to offer a link with one of the most annoying characters in *Star Trek* – Wesley Crusher.

The pompous combination of Wesley Wyndam-Pryce suggests a privileged upbringing in England and noble family. In England, last names are sometimes hyphenated among the privileged class, mostly to preserve storied or illustrious names that might otherwise be lost through marriage or to show off the eminence of both sets of family roots.

In England the Windhams (with various spellings) have been statesmen and military leaders. Descended from Normans of the Norman conquest, the family held an ancient seat in Wymondham in Norfolk. Their motto "au bon droit," "with good right," suggests being born to privilege. (*House of Names*)

The name "Pryce" suggests the weak new Watcher on *Buffy* is for sale – and so he is. He betrays Faith and Angel to the Watcher's Council, not for money, but because he has yet to develop personal ethics outside his training. Pryce actually comes from the Welsh "ap-Rhys" (son of Rhys) (*House of Names*). While the Normans were the privileged class, Welsh were oppressed for centuries and forbidden to learn their language and culture. Wesley's mixed name suggests he's not as privileged as first appears, and his abusive father reveals the same. Rhys means Ardor. Upon his arrival, Wesley certainly displays enthusiasm and love for his work, but must learn to supplement this with wisdom and judgment.

Winifred "Fred" Burkle/Illyria

Winifred is an old-fashioned countrified name (and Fred often uses expressions like "ain't" to underscore her Texas small town origins). In Welsh, it means "blessed peacemaking," which is certainly her role on the show.

Winifred is a whimsical name, much like the sweet, slightly mad character: In *Once Upon a Mattress*, Princess Winifred sings the song "A Girl Named Fred," and insists she must be called "Fred" not "Winnie." Winifred Foster is the heroine of *Tuck Everlasting*, and the Disney creators used it in *Jungle Book, Mary Poppins* and *Hocus Pocus.*

However, the *Angel* character is most often known as Fred, a gender-crossing name that causes confusion on first acquaintance (as seen when Angel is bodyswapped in "Carpe Noctem," A3.4). On *Buffy*, Andrew notes that Willow has a call from "Somebody named Fred. Guy sounds kinda effeminate" ("Lies My Parents Told Me," B7.17). Whedon often uses gender-flipped names, just as he assigns traditional gender roles to unexpected characters. Fred, like "Will" and Dana, is another androgynously named Final Girl, in contrast with the more feminine Buffy, Cordelia, and Jules. In fact, the practical and shy Fred survives sexy Cordelia's death, though not by very long.

Her last name, which may sound light and jokey, is even more masculine. It's a respelling of South German Bürkle, from a pet form of the name *Burkhard.* This name actually is comprised of "burg" (fort or castle) and "hard" (hardy, brave, strong).

When rescued from Pylea, Fred doesn't need naming, but has in fact forgotten her identity.

> CORDY: Who's there? What do you want?
> FRED: I forget. It's not important. ("Over the Rainbow," A2.20)

In the next episode, "Through the Looking Glass" (A2.21), Angel gives Fred her name back: Angel reads her California driver's license and tell her her name is "Winifred." He adds, "You're the girl from Cordy's vision!" and "They called you Fred. You were studying to be a physicist." Thus he gives her her name, occupation, nickname and origin, symbolically reconstructing her as a person before bringing her home.

Upon arrival, she's as mixed up and confused as her gender-swapped name, writing her life story and knowledge on the wall in an attempt to define herself.

St. Winifred of Wales made a private vow of chastity, and was murdered by a chieftain named Caradog of Hawarden whom she rejected. Saint Beuno raised her back to life and cursed Caradog, who was swallowed by the earth. Legend says that where her head fell, a well sprang up which became a place of pilgrimage, and whose waters were reported to heal leprosy, skin diseases, and other ailments. Her plot of dying and resurrecting in another form certainly fits the *Angel* character's arc. Her murderer (Knox) is killed and her new form is far more powerful than her simple human one.

In the final season of *Angel,* she changes into Illyria, a god who's outlived her followers and cannot discover her place in the world. Even more confusingly, she can become Fred at will, continuing to straddle expectations.

Illyria was an ancient region of the Balkans, lost after being conquered by the Roman Empire. As such, it harkens back to a pre-Western time, before the predominate culture erased more ancient civilizations. Shakespeare created "The Kingdom of Illyria" for his play *Twelfth Night.* This is a mysterious land, one in which the heroine feels friendless and alone, much like Illyria in Wolfram and Hart. The land of Illyria is also the setting of Lloyd Alexander's *The Illyrian Adventure,* the tale of Vesper Holly, a wealthy orphan and genius who goes on delightful adventures and a possible parallel for Fred.

According to Greek mythology, Illyria is named for Illyrius, who in some variants of the tale, is the son of Cadmus and Harmonia. The latter was the daughter of the war god Ares and queen of the Amazons, a fitting connection for the all-powerful Illyria. A later version of the myth identifies the monstrous Cyclops Polyphemus and Galatea, an artificially created woman, as the parents of Illyrius.

But Cadmus and Harmonia quitted Thebes and went to

the Encheleans. As the Encheleans were being attacked by the Illyrians, the god declared by an oracle that they would get the better of the Illyrians if they had Cadmus and Harmonia as their leaders. They believed him, and made them their leaders against the Illyrians, and got the better of them. And Cadmus reigned over the Illyrians, and a son Illyrius was born to him. But afterwards he was, along with Harmonia, turned into a serpent and sent away by Zeus to the Elysian Fields. (Apollodorus 3.5.4)

They say that the country received its name from Illyrius, the son of Polyphemus; for the cyclops Polyphemus and his wife, Galatea, had three sons, Celtus, Illyrius, and Galas, all of whom migrated from Sicily; and the nations called Celts, Illyrians, and Galatians took their origin from them. Among the many myths prevailing among many peoples this seems to me the most plausible. (Appian)

Thus Illyria the Merciless, God-King of the Primordium is a monster-hybrid from ancient times, or a lost civilization. As she walks through the law firm, she hearkens back to the primordial power they take for granted in their daily lives.

Buffy Movie

Lothos

This name is obviously derived from "loathe." Loathe, meaning "detest" and loath, "reluctant," come from the same Old English root word, lað, "hostile." Lothos is all three, as movie-Buffy is reluctant to face her destiny and battle the vampire king, a hostile force whom she detests.

He also represents her inner change of adolescence. "It's time to put away childish things," Lothos tells her.

After the graveyard [where she stakes her first vampire], Buffy wears a gothic white nightgown with a red ribbon in her hair, and dreams she's lying in the vampire king Lothos's arms; she's trying to break through to a higher consciousness. White is the color of untried maidenhood, while the brilliant red of blood, sexuality, and violence is

the realm of the grown woman. ... Young Buffy's
reaching out to be sexual, powerful, independent, though
it's all in the safety of her room and her dreams. (Frankel,
Buffy 14-15)

This, like kissing a frog in a fairytale, is another
"loathsome" moment – embracing the monster and facing
sexuality's dark side, as she will again with Angelus.

Merrick

Merrick is a Welsh variant of Maurice. Maurice means
"dark" according to some and "fame" and "power"
according to others. Merrick is indeed heir to fame and
power, but only through his duty as a Watcher, which
finally compels him to sacrifice himself. He labors under a
"dark" fate with dark premonitions of the war to come.
After his death, Buffy goes through her own dark night of
the soul in the original script and Buffy comic adaptation:
though she tries to pray, it quickly turns personal:

> I'm supposed to say something, but you're just dead. So
> totally dead, and I don't know what to do. You were the
> one who...I don't know if the training was over...I don't
> even know if I passed! How could you be so stupid?
> What am I going to do without you? ("Buffy: The Origin")

Without her Watcher's fame and power, she succumbs to
the darkness he warned her of.

Pike

As Buffy notes in the movie, "Pike isn't a name. It's a fish."
Pike is the slacker-boyfriend of the film, whom Buffy
loathes and then comes to appreciate. As a hot bad boy, he
has more than a trace of Spike in him; in the way the movie
Buffy was the-not-quite-realized show Buffy, Pike is a
sympathetic rebel who values a strong woman – a
precursor to Spike. They act, dress, and look similar: flask,
leather jacket, motorcycle, rebellion. "[Pike] was a guy
who'd let his girl do what she needed to do, and would
never judge her for being a little unladylike about the way

she went about it," comments author Seanan McGuire (18). Spike and Pike both have unusual nicknames. Pike may be a fish, but like Spike it's a medieval weapon, the pikestaff. Thus it's a phallic symbol as well as a powerful tool for Buffy to use in her war with the vampires.

Pike also has Xander parallels, as he must stake his best friend and he is the "damsel in distress" in the film, in contrast with Buffy the hero. As such, he's something of a useless flopping fish.

Buffy Allies and Villains

Adam

Adam is the Frankenstein character of the series, constructed from bits by a mad scientist. Mary Shelly actually intended her original monster to go by "Adam," so this name is fitting. With a religious, patriarchal name, he's also framed as part of the establishment. He sets himself up as leader and uniter of the monsters, until Buffy defeats him with her own particular magic and the power of friendship.

Buffy dreams of Adam as human in "Restless" (B4.22). He and Riley are naming everything, a self-important bureaucratic job that accomplishes nothing – Buffy by contrast acts and slays. It is also significant that Adam's job in the garden was to name all the animals; he's become the Biblical character and human.

> RILEY: Buffy, we've got important work here. A lot of filing, giving things names.
> BUFFY: (looks at other guy) What was yours?
> HUMAN-ADAM: Before Adam? Not a man among us can remember.

This may suggest Buffy must discover pre-Adamic mythology, and in fact, she spends the episode seeking the First Slayer, a powerful woman from before Judeo-Christian myth. Meanwhile, Adam has lost his earlier name, unsurprising for a collection of pieces. Just as Buffy became

59

more than herself by joining with her friends, Adam became less.

Amy Madison

Amy means "Dearly loved," an ironic commentary on her first appearance in "The Witch" (B1.3), in which her mother tries to steal her life from her. The use of first name Madison as a last name makes her seem particularly approachable and friendly as the team aids her, a friendliness that will prove problematic as she begins to corrupt Willow much later.

Dr. Angelman

This character works for the Initiative in season four. He obeys Walsh and her mission, echoing in some ways the Buffy-Angel relationship. However, his name appears to more directly follow Whedon's pattern of evil doctors and misguided true believers with Christian-inspired names.

Anne Steele/Chanterelle/Lily

This name-switching character is called Joan Appleby in the shooting script of "Lie to Me" (B2.7) though she calls herself Chanterelle. This is intriguing, as when Buffy names herself Joan in "Tabula Rasa" (B6.8) she's unknowingly linking herself with the other girl. Joan suggests Joan of Arc, emphasizing a hidden strength as well as a plain day-to-day name – the female equivalent to John and a last name for apple farmers. She runs from home, abandoning this identity, and allows others to name her, emphasizing how terribly lost she becomes.

> LILY: So how come you came up with Anne?
> BUFFY: It's my middle name.
> LILY: Lily's from a song. Rickie picked it. I'm always changing anyway. Chanterelle was part of my exotic phase.
> BUFFY: It's nice. It's a...it's a mushroom.
> LILY: It is? That's really embarrassing.
> BUFFY: Um, well, i-it's an exotic mushroom, if that's any comfort.

> LILY: Well, before that, I was following this loser preacher
> and calling myself "Sister Sunshine."
> BUFFY: What do they call you at home?
> Lily looks away and doesn't respond.
> BUFFY: I like Lily. ("Anne," B3.1)

The fact that she named herself (accidentally) for a mushroom suggests how ridiculous her life choices have become. The lily is a symbol of purity and resurrection, logical for a new identity, though also flimsy and defenseless. At episode end, she asks permission to name herself "Anne" after Buffy, as she decides to live on her own.

As Anne Steele, she's a social worker and the director of the East Hills Teen Center in Los Angeles. Using Buffy's name, she follows in her footsteps and resolves to protect innocents in danger. In the episode "Blood Money" (A2.12), Anne's driver's license lists her address as "Willoughby Ave." Anne Steele and John Willoughby are characters in Jane Austen's *Sense and Sensibility*. While this could be interpreted as a writer joke, it also suggests that the character deliberately faked name and address to copy a literary character – she's still mimicking others instead of being true to herself. Despite this, she helps Gunn reconcile with his long-discarded street side in the final episode.

> GUNN: What if I told you it doesn't help? What would you
> do if you found out that none of it matters? That it's all
> controlled by forces more powerful and uncaring than we
> can conceive, and they will never let it get better down
> here. What would you do?
> ANNE: I'd get this truck packed before the new stuff gets
> here.

Aphrodesia

"The new kid? She seems kind of weird to me. And what kind of name is Buffy?" Aphrodesia asks in the pilot. Her own name appears included to emphasize that she has no right to criticize. Aphrodesia is an exotic variant on Aphrodite, goddess of love, just as her friend Cordelia's name relates to the heart and Harmony's to peace. With

61

the last named member of the Cordettes called Aura, light, they have beautiful, graceful names for such a bunch of catty people.

April

April the robot is in many ways a precursor to the dolls of the Dollhouse, only designed to please others. As such, her name links with November and the other NATO names – she's an object and treated as such.

> Unlike Buffy, she's so selfless she's devoted her entire self to her boyfriend. Thus the parodic April comes off as a victim, a misogynistic fantasy gone wrong. Women shouldn't cry, she explains, that's manipulative. They should stay home and knit, be creative in bed, and have a one-sided selfless love that lasts forever. Further, in Warren's mind, they should turn off like a lamp when the boyfriend finds someone better and is ready to move on (Frankel, *Buffy* 120-121)

Of course, Warren, her creator, discovers like many Dollhouse clients that he actually wants someone real. "I mean, she's perfect. I don't know, I...I guess it was too easy. And predictable," Warren protests ("I Was Made to Love You," B5.15).

Ben Wilkinson

"Ben" as a syllable means "good" (as in, benign or benefit). And Ben is good, inside from the small matter of a selfish god inside him. Glory calls him "Gentle Ben," punning on the bear and his actual gentle nature. "Dawn sums up Ben's nature when, abducted as the key, she tells him that she prefers Glory because she does not pretend to be anything but a monster" (Jowett 134). His last name, derived from William, means "resolute protector," like the original name of his foe, Spike. Of course, he chooses to protect Glory rather than Dawn, thus causing Buffy's death.

Caleb

Caleb is deliberately an old-fashioned Biblical name,

representing his archaic sexist belief systems. In the Bible, Caleb is the skeptic who rejects tales that Canaan is filled with fantastical giants. He insists that he and his people can conquer the mysterious land, despite its threats. Caleb's plot on *Buffy* is similar. He rejects the concept of the powerful slayer and her potentials and sets out to prove they're only "dirty girls." While Biblical Caleb was a righteous man, and his name is given to many modern boys in religious families, the name melds Puritanical belief and skepticism.

He references the Bible extensively, showing through that and his priest clothing that he's part of the misogynistic religious establishment. In "Dirty Girls" (B7.18), Caleb says to Faith, "Well you're the other one. The Cain to her Abel. No offence to Cain, of course." He calls Buffy "the prodigal Slayer" in "Touched" (B7.20).

"My favorite villains are the ones you don't see coming," says Nathan Fillion, as he outlines the philosophy behind his chilling portrayal of Caleb in the closing episodes of Buffy. "What I enjoyed about playing Caleb was that he was so very, very clever, so very, very sweet, and so very, very twisted. I liked that he's not a typical villain. He's soft and sweet and righteous, and yet he's perverted and twisted in his head!" (*Dreamwatch*).

Chao-Ahn
Chao-Ahn is the Potential Slayer who only speaks Cantonese, resulting in several comedic gaffs. In Chinese, the names mean "Surpassing" and "Tranquil" though she becomes a courageous fighter, not a force of peace.

Clem
Clem is a yokel name from the countryside, suggesting his banality and harmlessness. In addition, "the kindly demon Clem is named for mercy, clemency" (Wilcox, *Why Buffy Matters* 50). He's kind towards others, and he's one of the first demons Buffy acknowledges as a person. In the comics, he goes on to be Harmony's best pal, offering her

the kindliness that she needs to balance her amorality.

Drusilla and Darla

Drusilla and Darla are in many ways shadows of each other with their feminine "D" names. Both are corrupters of their men, an image of vampire domesticity, and incestuous temptation for Angel and Spike. Both were introduced as enemies for Buffy and emotional pulls for Angel. Darla was a prostitute, whose name was lost to time. She is Angel's vampire mother and as such tries to guilt him into returning to his former savagery.

Drusilla, by contrast, is Angel's daughter. She, unusually among vampires, has kept her original name. She is not Angel's corrupter but corruptee, the "worst thing he ever did," as he tells Buffy in "Lie to Me" (B2.7). Angel adds later, "It was over the moment I saw her. She was my opposite in every way. Dutiful daughter. Devout Christian. Innocent and unspoiled. I took one look at her and I knew. She'd be my masterpiece," in the comic *Daddy Issues.*

Drusilla is defined by her love for Spike in every appearance on *Buffy*, especially her early ones. Darla, however, was a prostitute who insists "God never did anything for me" ("Darla"). She rejoices in holy wars, admitting she was never capable of love ("Lullaby," 3.9A).

While Drusilla has a distinct personality in her many namesakes through Roman history and Victorian literature, Darla simply means the generic "dear one." Unlike Drusilla, who keeps her original name, Darla's human name has been lost, and she allows the Master to name her. "What did you bring back? Did you bring back that girl, whose name I can't remember? Or did you bring back something else? The other thing," she asks, despairing ("Darla," A2.7). Namelessness and being named by others signifies a loss of identity or helpless service to the patriarchy in the cases of Anya, Lily, and others. Poor Darla takes her place among them, as she sacrifices herself for the good of her son.

On *Angel,* ironically, it is Darla who began the chain of

corruption, who has a chance for absolution. She is resuscitated as human, and Angel offers his life to give her a second chance. It's revealed much later that the life he bought in the trial wasn't hers but Connor's, their miracle baby. Drusilla steals Darla's humanity, but she reclaims it while pregnant with Connor. Darla in fact gives her life to save her human child, and her final appearance (excepting the flashback of "The Girl in Question," A5.20) is as Connor's guardian angel and ethical guide – she has become a higher being through her arc.

Drusilla, whose story begins as a saintly girl committed to holy orders, turns monstrous after her time on *Buffy*. She transforms the repentant human Darla into a vampire against her will, then tries to help Spike prey on humans in "Crush" (B5.14). In the *Angel and Faith* comic *Daddy Issues*, she becomes the Mother Superior – apparently sane but in fact a corrupter of others as she cripples them by absorbing their pain.

The name Drusilla is quite old-fashioned, more Victorian (appropriate to her birth era) than modern. Literary characters from that era named Drusilla appear in Thomas Hardy's *Jude the Obscure,* Wilkie Collins's *The Moonstone* and Faulkner's *The Unvanquished.* In her first appearances on *Buffy*, she lounges about in an ethereal white gown, an anachronism from the romantic past to contrast with the modern, assertive Buffy.

> Drusilla (whose very name is flowery) plants daisies, sings to a lost little boy, and teases her pet bird in exaggerated girly fashion. However, these encounters are tainted, as daisies and bird are dead and boy soon will be if Drusilla has her way. Everything around her is corrupted and twisted, from the bloody heart she gets for Valentine's Day to the dollies she gags with red ribbon and punishes. While Buffy is a defender of life, Drusilla is death, both its bringer and its victim, as she is forever cut off from her former sanity and potential. (Frankel, *Buffy* 51)

Drusilla's Bible namesake was an immoral woman and

an adulterer who unrepentantly ran off with a brute. As such, she corresponds well to the *Buffy* character. Drusilla is an ancient Roman name, meaning fruitful or "dewy-eyed." Of course, she never bears children, and her fruitful imagination is a place of only madness.

Forrest Gates

Having a character named Forrest in the military may suggest Forrest Gump, but in the season where Buffy is "lost in the woods," confused by college and dressing like Little Red Riding Hood, his name emphasizes that she doesn't fit among the Initiative. "Gates" similarly suggest a locked door with Forrest as its doorkeeper. Indeed, he resents Buffy for the way she's enticing Riley's loyalties away from the Initiative.

Glory/Glorificus

Glorificus does not sound glorious as a name – it sounds somewhat more monstrous, like "Tyrannosaurus." Thus when this name is used, she resembles a gargantuan monster. The name Glory is ironic – she is not a glorious god but instead petty and selfish. She's willing to destroy the entire world only to go home. She tortures innocents to feed off them.

When Giles first researches her, he tellingly has trouble finding her name. As he says in "No Place Like Home" (B5.5), "All we've managed to uncover so far is the Dagon Sphere was created to repel That Which Cannot Be Named. ... Anything that goes unnamed is usually an object of deep worship or great fear – maybe both." Professor Janet Brennan Croft notes:

> In "Shadow" (B5.8), Giles, Tara, and Willow speculate that the reason they cannot find a name for her in their books is that she "pre-dates the written word [...] predates language itself." If this is true, Glorificus is probably not her actual name—more likely it is a title. -*ficus* is a Latin suffix which might be interpreted as meaning "making, causing, producing," "performing

actions of a certain kind," or "bringing into a specified state" (OED). She prefers her minions to call her Glory, and glory of a certain twisted and destructive sort is what she sees herself as causing, producing, or becoming.

Glorificus is a monster with a monster's name, though "Glory" is somewhat less, buttered up through her many nicknames and titles: "most beauteous and supremely magnificent one," "most tingly and wonderful Glorificus," "shiny special one," "your elaborate marvelousness," "your creamy coolness," and so on ("Shadow," B5.8).

Especially with the nicknames above, Glory is "a parodic version of the overdressed blonde bimbo some have considered Buffy. As such she is an appropriate foe for Buffy to defeat prior to her rebirth" (Wilcox, "Who Died and Made Her the Boss?" 17). She's a shadow of Buffy, her selfishness brought to life. "I'm in pain!" she hollers in "Intervention" (B5.18), and her minions rush to comfort her with chocolates and beautiful red dresses, just as Buffy is shrouding herself in brown and concentrating only on the mission. "I am great and I am beautiful, and when I walk into a room all eyes turn to me, because my name is a holy name..." Glory smirks arrogantly. She calls Buffy "Mousy the Vampire Slayer." "You may be tiny queen in vampire world, but to me, you're a bug," she tells Buffy. "You should get down on your knees and worship me!" ("Checkpoint," B5.12). Buffy literally and metaphorically defeats her through a selfless act – giving her life to save Dawn.

Halfrek/Cecily
Cecily actually means blind, named after the famously blind Saint Cecilia. Certainly, the lady is willfully blind as she ignores William Pratt's interest in her.

> SPIKE: I love you, Cecily.
> CECILY: Please stop!
> SPIKE: I know I'm a bad poet but I'm a good man and all I ask is that... that you try to see me–
> CECILY: I do see you. That's the problem. You're nothing

to me, William. You're beneath me. ("Fool for Love," B5.7)

He even begs that she try to "see" him, but she refuses.

Halfrek appears to recognize Spike in "Older and Far Away" (B6.14) – she calls him William, and he recognizes her as well. The same actress plays both and it's certainly possible that Cecily was spurned in love and became a vengeance demon. Her name divides into half-wreck...apparently that's what she does upon entering a situation – she half-wrecks it.

Harmony Kendall

The name means peaceful unity, named as it is after the goddess Harmonia. Mostly this is ironic, as even while human, she tends to stir up trouble, from insulting Buffy and her friends to turning on Cordelia when she becomes interested in Xander.

After becoming a vampire, she becomes even more annoying. On *Angel,* Wesley points out that "Harm" is a perfect nickname for her, and the episode names "Disharmony" and "Harm's Way" emphasize the connection. The comics "Harmonic Divergence" "Harmony Comes to the Nation" and "In Perfect Harmony" are little better, as Harmony preys on humanity, then successfully turns her activities into a reality show. As she puts it, "You got a hero with a villain built in." While on the reality show, she appears a force for good, she's actually increasing hate and violence in the world.

Kendall is a place name from "Kendale," "the valley of the River Kent." With a river name, Harmony is associated with the feminine, though her last name sounds like Ken-doll for a gender crossover or tie to frivolous Barbie. To emphasize this, Willow calls Kennedy ken-doll in the comics.

India Cohen

According to the novels, and possibly other sources, India Cohen immediately preceded Buffy Summers as the Slayer.

Her last name is a classic Jewish one, suggesting her religion and also an ancient tie to the priesthood. Slayers, especially Buffy with her cross, appear to be instruments of God's will fighting the unclean plague of demons to defend the innocent.

The name India links with the exotic, far-off country. India became popular as a first name during British imperialism, generally to show support for the colonization of the subcontinent. Thus India herself may be British and Jewish. India literally means "body of water" (the Indus River) suggesting the origin of all life as well as feminine water magic. In at least one of the novels, her ghost returns to aid Buffy in an epic battle. It's actually surprising that on seven seasons of *Buffy*, plus the movie and comics, Buffy's predecessor, who died to make her slayer, is never referenced.

Jenny Calendar/Janna of the Kalderash

This character begins in "I Robot, You Jane" (B1.8) with a nondescript name – Jenny is an incredibly popular American name, and Calendar may reference the school calendar, among other things. (She may also be Giles's destined love and personal calendar girl.) Jennifer is an adaptation of Guinevere, casting her as Giles's romantic partner, and, eventually, his weakness. However, the writers realized that knowing so little about her offered opportunities and by "Surprise" (B2.13) she was revealed to be hiding the truth in plain sight: She is actually Janna of the Kalderash, one of the Romany sent to watch Angel.

Jana is the Islamic name for paradise (a chilling foreshadowing). It's also a variant of Diana, goddess of the hunt, emphasizing her tracking of Angel and protecting of Buffy, as Diana was the eternal virgin who demanded the same from her maidens. From the Biblical roots, Janna means "the one who speaks or answers," and in fact, Janna knows the key to Angel's curse and reveals all to Buffy (too late) in "Innocence" (B2.14).

Her name is also a variant on Janos, the two-faced god

from "Halloween" (B2.6). She becomes a figure of deceit and mistrust on the show, emphasizing her double identity. "Each time there's a twisted prophecy, Jenny Calendar appears. For she's the mystery woman, knower and manipulator of all that's secret" (Frankel, *Buffy* 60). She enjoys lying, constructing a complex tale of defacing Giles's prized first edition because, as she says flirtatiously, "I just love to see you squirm" ("The Dark Age," B2.8).

> She's the only one of Buffy's allies ever taken over by a demon personality (excluding the vampires). When this happens, the demon wears her face, casting Jenny as deceitfulness incarnate below her human surface. In "Surprise" (2.13), she's revealed as a double agent, who's concealed her exotic name and gypsy "otherness" as well as her agenda. As she lies clumsily and lures Buffy into her car, viewers expect the worst. Ominous music swells. Of course, she's only taking Buffy to her surprise party, where Jenny finds a justifiable excuse to decoy Angel out of town, but in this moment, Jenny is revealed as a figure of mistrust and uncertain loyalty. In "Innocence" (2.14), a devastated Buffy dreams of Jenny, veiled, standing by a grave. Jenny not only knows why Angel became a monster but partially caused it by keeping secrets. (Frankel, *Buffy* 60)

Even after her death, she appears as the First in "Amends" (B3.10) to torment Angel into committing suicide, as he nearly does. As such, she is mystery woman and deceiver, down to her exotic name and background.

Kakistos
This demon's name means "worst" in Greek and he's said to be "the worst of the worst." He kills Faith's watcher and comes for her as well. Buffy, with her habit of demystifying evil, calls him "Kissing Toast" and "Taquitos."

Kathy Newman
Kathy Newman appears in "The Freshman" and "Living Conditions" (B4.1-4.2) as Buffy's roommate at UC Sunnydale. Newman is like a synonym for freshman. Kathy

means pure and Kathy seems pure in her interests and devotion to Cher. Of course, she's also pure demon.

Kendra Young

Kendra is Anglo-Saxon for prophetess. Slayers get prophetic dreams, and Kendra's death also foreshadows Buffy's in season five, and Angel's trip to hell. She may also be named for Kendra Saunders, Hawkgirl. Other fascinatingly appropriate name meanings include "knowledge" and "greatest champion." Of course, Kendra lacks experience, relying simply on book-learning, which cannot save her. Her last name of course emphasizes her youth before her untimely death. While her accent is exotic and she's one of the show's few nonwhite characters, her two names are traditional British, suggesting a kinship with Giles, who appreciates her scholarship.

Kennedy

Kennedy is a much more popular last name than first. It actually means "helmet head; ugly head" in Gaelic, suggesting war rather than romance. As a Potential who's also a lesbian, Kennedy manages to achieve both as she's actually far from ugly. No last name is given in the show or comics. As her story goes on, she brings Buffy and Willow an attitude that they must fight for others not themselves, reflecting President Kennedy's "Ask not what your country can do for you; ask what you can do for your country."

Miss Kitty Fantastico

Miss Kitty Fantastico, Tara and Willow's pet cat, has a colorful, self-important name. Her owners are being whimsical and sweet, but there's more symbolism in "Restless" (B4.22) when Tara mentions cats can take care of themselves (presumably like Slayers). In "End of Days" (B7.21), Dawn says, "I don't leave crossbows around all willy-nilly. Not since that time with Miss Kitty Fantastico." It's unclear what actually happened, but the cat hasn't been seen in years.

71

Larry Blaisdell
Larry Blaisdell, a student at Sunnydale High in Seasons Two and Three, is played by Larry Bagby III. His first name presumably comes from his actor's, while the last name unfortunately means "stutter" – as it turns out, Larry's outward confidence hides a deep insecurity.

Maggie Walsh
Critics have noted that Walsh is a Margaret Thatcher figure, perfectly represented by the nickname Maggie (Wilcox, *Why Buffy Matters* 48). While a powerful woman, she also serves the patriarchy as part of its militaristic hierarchy. Walsh is an Irish surname, meaning "foreigner," or literally "Welshman." Maggie Walsh is a foreign invader to the military world of the Initiative and the magical world of the Slayer (to say nothing of the demon world!). While she struggles to rule over all these groups, she is ultimately unsuccessful. Her "son" Adam, a real patchwork outsider, inducts her into his own group by remaking her as a zombie.

The Master/Mayor/Judge
The unnamed Master and Judge are figures of the patriarchy. The Master is the father of the Darla-Angel-Drusilla-Spike line, and the vampire king of Buffy's first season. He's technically the only character to kill Buffy (as she jumps in season five). His identity of simply "Master" makes him seem faceless and all-powerful. The Judge is much the same.

> As Angelus schemes to destroy Buffy's life, he starts with the mall, home to Buffy's daylight world of innocent people and frivolous shopping. When Buffy arrives, Angelus stands with the broken Drusilla at his side. Between them is the Judge, a heartless figure of male rule whose touch "can literally burn the humanity out of you." This is a chilling trio of death for stunned, sorrowing Buffy to face. However, Buffy is a model of female empowerment. She hauls out the rocket launcher and fires straight into the Judge's chest. Confronted by her

> fearless will, he shatters. Angelus and Drusilla fly over the railing. (Frankel, *Buffy* 69-70)

The Mayor, generally called simply by his title, fills the identical role. As he condescends to Buffy and molds Faith into a wholesome, milk-drinking girl in a pink summer dress, he establishes himself as the man in charge. His name, Richard Wilkins III, sounds like a pompous politician's. At the same time, his first name means "hard ruler," and the second is yet another "will," suggesting he will be a difficult opponent as well as patriarch.

Quentin Travers
Quentin is a Latin name for fifth, emphasizing the old-world establishment and its preoccupation with hierarchy. The last name comes from a toll-keeper from the Old English related to "traverse." He is the establishment, the government representative, and most importantly the barrier on Buffy's activities. Significantly, Travers and the Watcher's Council are the "toll" Buffy must pay for being a Slayer, and she finds a way to work with them in "Checkpoint" (B5.12).

Parker Abrams
Buffy sleeps with him and wishes she hadn't. Parker is a surname name, meaning "keeper of the park." A surname for first name suggests distance, while the meaning makes him "keeper of the college," with the power to welcome or reject Buffy, as indeed he does. Abrams is a variant on Abraham – the Biblical patriarch and a representation of the patriarchy in general – an unenlightened caveman, as shown in "Beer Bad" (B4.4).

Rack
Rack the drug-dealing warlock clearly uses a nickname. It's a hard, masculine sounding name. In fact, he sells racks of drugs in a type of racket.

Robert "Bob" Flutie

Flutie is the principal of Sunnydale High School until he's eaten by possessed students. While disliked, deliberately distant Snyder has no name given, Flutie wants students to feel comfortable calling him Bob, as he says. Robert means "bright fame," and he's referenced occasionally after his death...though it's unlikely he hoped to be famous for being eaten. Flutie is a frivolous, laughable last name.

Robin Wood

Robin Wood is named for film critic Robin Wood, whom Whedon admires. At the same time, "Robin" comes from Robert, "bright fame," suggesting Wood's skill and talented future ahead as a rare male slayer (of a sort). "Wood" links his name with Spike, his vicious shadow and the man who made him what he is. Buffy is lost in the woods, unable to face her season seven enemies, until Robin brings her insight with the Emergency Slayer Kit.

Sineya

This name is given to the First Slayer in the comics. In "Restless" (B4.22) she's known only as the Primitive, mute and nameless in a way that usually reflects weakness in the characters. In Buffy's "Restless" dream, modern, mystical Tara must speak for her: "I have no speech. No name. I live in the action of death, the blood cry, the penetrating wound. I am destruction. Absolute...alone." Upon hearing this description, Buffy knows she's "The Slayer."

As a word, Sineya is a region in Kouroussa, Guinea, on Africa's West coast. Like Melaka Fray, Sineya has a place name, associating her with the land. Aside from being a simplistic, exotic, and feminine name, it comes from the cradle of man and the place where the Slayer line began.

Principal R. Snyder

While Snyder is Dutch for tailor, it sounds like the English "snide" and "sly," appropriate tags for the evil principal. In contrast to Flutie who says students should feel free to call him "Bob," Snyder is never given a first name, only an initial on his desk, thus dehumanizing him.

Veruca
Veruca, the selfish werewolf who encourages Oz to act out, most likely is named for the selfish Veruca Salt in Roald Dahl's *Charlie and the Chocolate Factory.* She in turn is named for a wart, stressing the unappealing nature of the character.

Vi
Vi (or Violet) is Potential who joins the group in "Showtime" (B7.11), played by Felicia Day. While timid on the show, at first, she grows to lead the New York Slayer squadron by the season eight comics (*Time of Your Life,* B8.4). Violets are associated with shyness, and offer another flower name, though the nickname Vi sounds a bit more assertive and independent.

Warren Meers, Jonathan Levinson and Andrew Wells
The trio have ordinary boys' names, emphasizing the prosaic nature of their threat. "Meers" even sounds like "merely" – he is a merely human opponent, not a vampire. Buffy's "arch-nemesises...ses" are indisputably the boys next door, the ones with whom Buffy and her friends went to school.

It's the Trio's banality that emphasizes how Buffy's life has changed. "Buffy, you used to create these grand villains to battle against, and now what is it? Just ordinary students you went to high school with. No gods or monsters – just three pathetic little men who like playing with toys," the doctor comments in the self-referential episode "Normal Again" (B6.17). "In a season where about leaving childish things behind and taking responsibility, the perfect villains are ones who can't," Espenson notes, as the Trio collect action figures and squabble ("Life is the Big Bad").

Their names are horribly ironic, as Warren means "protecting friend" and Andrew means "manly" – both are anything but. Jonathan in the Bible was a true friend to King David and a revolutionary among the Maccabees. His name means "God has given." This Jonathan, by contrast, is all-too normal, and every advantage he's "given" is taken away in "Superstar" (B4.17).

Whistler

The concept of whistling in the dark – challenging the mystical unknown and the status quo – certainly embodies Whistler. In fact, his name wasn't created from nothing. In the comic and movie *Blade*, Blade, a vampire slayer, has a mentor named Whistler – Angel's Whistler is clearly an homage. Whistler was intended to set Angel on his path once more at the beginning of his own series (though Doyle got the job instead). Despite this absence, Whistler appears in the comics as well, to give Angel his role as Twilight, then appoint his successors who will bring balance by empowering the demons.

Xin Rong

Xin Rong (called Chinese Slayer on the show) was killed by Spike in the Boxer Rebellion. While she only appears in "Fool for Love" (B5.7), she introduces herself in the *Spike & Dru* comic "All's Fair." Xinrong means "serious" and "stable," while the Chinese phrase *xin xin xiang rong* means thriving and flourishing grass and plants. While her name suggests she's the lifeforce incarnate, Spike tragically cuts it short.

Angel Allies and Villains

Allen Francis Doyle

As is true with all of Whedon's creations, the name of the character serves as a type of map to the inner world of the character. "Doyle" is an Irish family name meaning "dark foreigner" (Doyle). This is a perfect moniker for this character, who fits the classic "black Irish" type of black hair and light eyes, and who is also very much a stranger in the strange land of Los Angeles. In addition to being a "foreigner" in the world of full humans, Doyle is also a stranger to the ways and means of redemption. (Koontz, "The One That Almost Got Away")

It's revealed in "The Bachelor Party" (A1.7) that Doyle's Brachen demon side only appeared when he turned 21. He promptly quit his job teaching third grade, and probably his volunteering at the food bank as well.

Notably, he also changes his name at this point, casting off his given (and slightly prissy) name of "Francis," a name that calls up images of the gentle, kind St. Francis, in favor of being the one-name, more masculine-sounding "Doyle," the dark foreigner. Far from being an active, vibrant force for good in the world by teaching children and assisting the hungry, the now angry-at-the-world Doyle retreats from human companionship. (Koontz, "The One That Almost Got Away")

As with Angel in "Becoming" (B2.22), Doyle was descending into darkness, until he found a purpose – in this case, helping Angel save those in need. However, his Francis side and Doyle side continue to war within him. Alan, from the Gaelic "ailin," little rock, represents his steadiness as well as the Catholic church and the rock on which it was founded. Francis means "Frenchman," another name that means foreigner, though it also offers religious implications as generous St. Francis of Assisi.

In "The Bachelor Party" (1.7), Doyle single-handedly rescues Cordelia from a vampire attack after Cordelia's pretty-boy date has turned tail and fled. Beaten badly himself, his first question is to Cordelia – "Are you okay?" Clearly, he is closer to being the volunteering "Francis" of old than the wheeler-dealer "Doyle" of Los Angeles.

He dies in the aptly named "Hero" (A1.9), saving innocent part-demons from an extremist hate group, finally finding the children's teacher and selfless saint in himself on the moment of his death.

Dana

Dana is the mad slayer seen in "Damage" (A5.11) confined in a psychiatric hospital. Her name comes from Daniel, "God is my judge," but she actually acts as judge and executioner for Spike, who sadly points out afterwards that it was fair – he killed and tortured many people, even if she wasn't one of them. By contrast, Dana in *Cabin in the Woods* is the most sensible, stable character.

Daniel Holtz

Daniel in the Bible performs a great feat of courage – the king hurls him into a lion's den and he survives, for God protects him and shuts the lions' mouths. Daniel Holtz is also brave, as a vampire hunter centuries in the past. He is also subjected to great torment, as Angelus retaliates by killing his family. However, Biblical Daniel is protected by God and goes on to become a great leader after his ordeal. Holtz pursues violence and finally kills himself so that Angel will take the blame for it.

His name means "God is my judge." However, Daniel Holtz ignores this message. He becomes a judge on his own, bring divine retribution down on Angel for his past. Of course, he ignores Angel's ensoulment, establishing that he seeks revenge, not justice. His wife is Caroline, "free," suggesting her independent spirit until Angelus finds her. Holtz is a German surname, meaning forest – he is in fact the fairytale monster of the story, sent to destroy Angel.

David Nabbit

David Nabbitt is a wealthy software developer who wants to be on Angel's team, complete with purple cape. Nabbit, a play on "nab" and "rabbit," is a character in *New Super Mario Bros. U.* However, those who discount him should reread the story of David from the Bible, who slew a giant monster though he wasn't a warrior. Perhaps Angel should reconsider. Cordy tells him: "I like David. It's such a strong, masculine name. It just feels – good in your mouth" ("War Zone," A1.20). Though her quip is embarrassingly awkward, she hints at his potential to become more than the "big nerd" she calls him earlier.

Dennis Pearson

This is Cordelia's ghost, whom she calls "The Phantom Dennis" at one point, punning on *The Phantom Menace.* "Dennis" actually comes from Dionysius, Greek god of wine and drunken chaos. Between this namesake and *Dennis the Menace*, the character is set up as the perfect poltergeist though Cordelia seems to like him.

Drogyn

A mystic warrior who has lived for at least a thousand years, Drogyn guards the Deeper Well, and cannot lie. His name echoes "dragon," famed as mystical guardians of treasures.

Eve

Eve shows up to tempt Angel in season five. She gives him an apple "to get the whole irony thing out of the way." He bites into it, and from that moment, begins to compromise his ethics ("Conviction," A5.1). As Wolfram and Hart's liaison, she's unsubtly linked with Biblical Eve. Angel and Eve's sexual encounter in "Life of the Party" (A5.5) also suggests an Adam and Eve moment as the villainess seduces the good hero. "Looks like we're getting kicked out of the garden, Eve," he says in their last episode, as Wolfram and Hart crumbles ("Why We Fight," A5.22).

Gavin Park

The name Gavin is a British variant of Gawain, Arthur's best knight, though given to selfish sinning on occasion. It means "Battle Hawk." Gavin is of course one of the top "knights" for Wolfram and Hart and a main competitor with Lilah Morgan – the Morgan le Fay character. His last name "Park" suggests civilization as opposed to wilderness – parks and greenhouses symbolize mankind's mastery over untamed nature. Gavin Park gains his advantages through legal maneuverings and paperwork in contrast with Lilah's mystical approach.

Groosalugg

> ANGEL: (Watching the Groosalugg stick his hand in open flame) This guy – he doesn't feel pain?
> FRED: Oh, he feels it, but – he's the Groosalugg. He overcomes all things. Good luck!

The champion of Pylea is introduced with his monstrous name (or rather title, as it's *the* Groosalugg) to frighten Cordelia. When she sees a monstrous demon whom she thinks she must mate with, she insists, "Kill me now." In fact, when she discovers he's a gorgeous self-deprecating human with solid blue eyes, she falls head over heels. She renames him the more approachable Groo and dresses him as Angel when he joins her on earth.

He may be named for Groo the Wanderer, a Conan parody. On one occasion, Groo the Wanderer is introduced with a fearsome description, only to disappoint when he shows up, short and scruffy. Thus the story emphasizes the Groosalugg's courage but also his ineptness to deal with life on earth without Cordelia to guide him. Still, like Groo the Wanderer, he maintains a cheerful optimism and stalwart bravery on his adventures.

Upon Angel's noting that Groo "had no problem pronouncing 'Pomegranate'" in "The Price" (A3.19), Groo responds, "It was my mother's name." This is a puzzling statement , considering Groo's origins in the demon realm of Pylea. Of course, putting aside the joke here, this is one of many nature names given to Whedon's female characters. Pomegranates are a symbol of motherhood with their many seeds inside. They also allude to the story of Persephone, in which a girl is stolen into hell and escapes, but because of the pomegranate seeds she ate, she must return each year. Cordelia, stolen into Pylea, has escaped, but her demon side is growing stronger through season three. Groo represents a choice between love and her ultimate destiny.

Gwen Raiden

This Catwoman-style thief meets the Angel team in "Ground State" (A4.2). After working with them in several episodes, she stays on in the comics, in which she dates Connor and sacrifices herself to save the team (though she comes back when time is corrected).

Gwen is a Welsh name meaning "white, holy," sometimes a shortened form of Gwenhwyfar (Guinevere). Her surname references Raiden, the Japanese god of thunder and lightning and the *Mortal Kombat* character Raiden, who could shoot lightning from his hands. Thus her name actually means "white lightning."

Holland Manners

> MANNERS: That's really the question you should be asking yourself, isn't it? See, for us, there is no fight. Which is why winning doesn't enter into it. We – go on – no matter what. Our firm has always been here. In one form or another. The Inquisition. The Khmer Rouge. We were there when the very first cave man clubbed his neighbor. See, we're in the hearts and minds of every single living being. And that – friend – is what's making things so difficult for you. See, the world doesn't work in spite of evil, Angel. It works with us. It works because of us. Welcome to the home office.
> ANGEL: This isn't...
> MANNERS: Well, you know it is. You know that better than anyone. Things you've seen. Things you've, well, done. You see, if there wasn't evil in every single one of them out there why, they wouldn't be people. They'd all be angels. Have a nice day. ("Reprise," A2.15)

Holland Manners, one of the highest-up at Wolfram and Hart, supervises Darla's resurrection, among other matters. His name, for the country, is from the Old Dutch *holt lant* ("wood land") suggesting a connection with where he rules, or a British surname for someone from Holland. His first name as surname is formal and distancing, while his last name of course smacks of "manners" and propriety. His final words are ones of bargaining and conciliation:

> MANNERS: Angel – please. – People are going to die.
> ANGEL: And yet, somehow, I just can't seem to care.
> [Manners' own words from earlier]
> MANNERS: Angel? P-please we can negotiate...
> ("Reunion," A2.10)

Darla feeds on him, and he dies. In 2002, the LAPD show *The Shield* launched. One character was Detective Holland "Dutch" Wagenbach, with a name possibly inspired by the *Angel* character.

The Immortal, the Beast, the Oracles

All of these gain a numinous mystery through their imposing namelessness. Of course, in the Immortal's case, it's something of a joke, and the Beast is not what it appears. The Oracles stand silently, judgingly apart from the world, until they are massacred and their godlike unapproachability is lost.

Jasmine

> FRED. I don't know. I can't imagine one word, you know, summing you up. I mean, you're a superior being. Shouldn't you – Don't you want to choose it yourself?
> WOMAN: No one born to this earth can choose their own name. They are named by those who love them. There are some rules even I must follow. ("Shiny Happy People," A4.18)

Though a powerful woman, Jasmine refuses to name herself. Of course, she is not strong in the way Buffy is strong, but only powerful through deceiving and using others. This may be an insidious hint, as she rules through subtlety and mind control, not by declaring her strength overtly. She also hints at the ancient magic that names are things of power when she cites the "rules," emphasizing the power behind her true name.

Several significant names are proposed after Fred

accidentally suggests calling her "Clorox" ("Shiny Happy People," A4.18). Gunn suggests "Helen," his grandmother's name but also the loveliest woman of all, Helen of Troy. Of course, she also killed thousands with her beguiling beauty. Wesley proposes Aristophila (which he defines as "supreme lover of mankind" but it actually means love of the aristocracy), Dianthia (divine flower) or Iphigenia. The last of these was sacrificed to save the men of Troy as a helpless victim. Ironically, Jasmine is instead the sacrificer. And if she loves mankind, she loves them for dinner.

As a night-blooming flower, Jasmine evokes imagery of vampires. The jasmine flower symbolizes love, modesty, sensuality, and attachment, and it was used as an aphrodisiac. Jasmine the character is in fact beloved, modest, and sensual – all who see her form an unhealthy attachment. In Menton it was believed that a husband who offered his bride jasmine would die within the year (Watts 213). In China the jasmine flowers are a symbol of happiness – again, this is true if far too literally.

The jasmine flower is also a symbol of the Virgin Mary (Watts 213) and thus functions with Whedon's religious names for villains like Caleb and symbols of the wicked establishment like Jubal Early or Dr. Matthias.

In "Sacrifice" (A4.20), Wesley meets a demon with a prior claim:

> WESLEY: Jasmine. That's what we call her.
> The...superior being that – that you loved first.
> DEMON: Pfah! You name her….She is the devourer, the song, the peace, the whole, and you try to name her!

Wesley and his friends have inadvertently claimed power over Jasmine by trying to define her. The demon continues to explain:

> DEMON: Mmm, this blood magic. Flesh magic. Older than words. More much power. This magic she will hear. She will hear and remember her true ones. … You creatures! Throwing your names all over all the time! That's why you're so weak. Too many are knowing your

names, takes your power away.
WESLEY: It doesn't work that way here. With us —
(beat) So that's the word, isn't it? The word she cares
about? [...] She has a name, and it has power over her!
That's why she keeps it a secret! [...] And somehow her
true name prevents her from choosing a false one? So
one of us had to do it.

This of course is the key to defeating her, even more than the magic of her blood. Though humans can slip in and out of names, hers is a tether, controlling as well as defining her.

Justine Cooper

Justine carries the root "just" as she partners with Daniel ("God is my judge") Holtz on his quest. The most famous Justine is the title character of the Marquis de Sade's novel entitled *Justine ou Les Malheurs de la vertu* (1791) (*Justine, or The Misfortunes of the Virtue*). Though she seeks to be good, Justine is raped by the monks with whom she seeks refuge, in the first of many similar encounters. Attempting to escape prison, she and her criminal confederate start a fire, killing 21 people. In short, she very much resembles Drusilla. It's revealed at the end that her sister, who choses vice, has a much better existence. Justine Cooper is likewise in quest of virtue, but is taken advantage of and fails to find it. Cooper is the Anglo-Saxon term for a barrel-maker, stressing Justine's traditional British origins.

Kate Lockley

Kate, short for Katherine, means pure. In fact, Kate Lockley is pure human, uncorrupted by the demon world or even knowledge of it before Angel drags her in. It can also mean virginal, and certainly, Angel and LAPD Detective Kate never find a perfect relationship. Lockley is a British place name, with the sound of lock to it, suggesting the jail cells and a belief in proper order.

Lilah Morgan

Lilah is frequently a liar, emphasized by the first syllable of her name. She also references this concept in the show:

> WESLEY: It's a lie!
> LILAH: Lah. It's a Lilah ("Home," A4.22).

Her name is Hebrew for night, reminding watchers of the dark side she represents. As such, she represents the shadowy world of the unconscious and violent impulses (Chevalier and Gheerbrant 608). Night is "associated with the mysterious darkness and the protection of the womb" (Biedermann 236). It was the sphere of women, but also a time of terror and witchcraft.

She shares name-roots with the night-demoness of Jewish culture, Lilith, the strong minded first wife of Eve who transforms into a demon and slayer of children. Lilah preys on the innocent in several episodes and functions as Wesley's evil impulse as love-interest in the late third season. In the Bible, "Lilith was to become the foe of Eve, promoting adultery and extramarital relationships" (Chevalier and Gheerbrant 608). She stood for a rejection of traditional marriage and family life. Of course, Wesley abandons "good" Fred and Cordelia for bad girl Lilah with whom he has a perverse and abusive relationship.

Her last name echoes Morgan le Fay, another famed dark temptress. Using dark spells or vicious wiles, she famously corrupts the good hero. Once again, her flirtation with Wesley and the series' other men, from Angel to Lindsey, reflects this connection. Morgan le Fay, some think, is in turn named for the Morrigan, Celtic goddess of war and death.

Lindsey McDonald

Lindsey is more often a girl's name than a boy's. Lindsey, notably, spends the series struggling to find his place in the world. While he begins as committed to Wolfram and Hart, his love for Darla complicates matters. Wolfram and Hart brings her back in emotional pain, with a terminal illness, and then turns her vampire against her will. When the firm's miraculous gift of a working hand is revealed as equally corrupt (with Lindsey's coworker harvested for his body parts!) Lindsey rejects the law firm and all it represents. His own hand is acting against him, emphasizing how fundamentally he's torn. He finally heads back to the country in his ancient truck, seeking the Lindsey from before L.A. As he returns to his roots in farmland, he becomes "Old McDonald" the farmer in truth.

His name means "island of linden trees," emphasizing his connection to place and nature. The linden was hallowed to the pre-Christian Germanic peoples, who would assemble and dance under a linden tree, but also hold their judicial meetings there –thus the Linden was a place of law and trials. Verdicts in rural Germany continued to be referred to as *sub tilia* (under the linden).

In the fifth season, he's an equally liminal figure, calling himself Doyle as he insists he's come to aid Spike in being a true champion. Clearly, he's trying a moment of wish-fulfillment – he longs to be the hero who died to save innocents, instead of the morally-ambiguous villain of the piece. He and Angel have switched places, as Angel is now the establishment of Wolfram and Hart, and Lindsey claims he's the solitary hero saving people on the streets.

Once again, of course, larger forces are at play, and once again, Angel strips away his pretense, revealing his true agenda. Shapeshifting, boundary-straddling Lindsey cannot be trusted, he is too slippery, too indoctrinated by the lawyers. To Lindsey's disgust, he is not elevated to either archvillain or hero – he is killed not by his great nemesis Angel but by pacifist Lorne.

Linwood Murrow
This Wolfram & Hart lawyer is president of the "Special Projects Division." The name means "Linden Tree Valley," another formal surname for a first name. Murrow is from the Old Gaelic for "warrior from the sea," a fierce name like Wolfram and Hart itself. Lilah's direct superior until she

kills him, his Li- name and linden tree link ties him to the scheming pair of Lilah and Lindsey.

Marcus Hamilton

Eve's replacement and a child of the senior partners, played by Adam Baldwin. He's tougher than Eve, remarking, "You don't really think you're gonna win this, do you? You don't stand a chance. We are legion. We are forever." In Latin, Marcus means Hammer. As the tool of the senior partners, with a name derived from the war god, Mars, Hamilton lives up to his name. His namesake, Marcus Antonius (Mark Antony), also fought a great war and lost, as Hamilton does to Angel. Hamilton is a place name from the Old English hamel "crooked, mutilated" and dun "hill." This Wolfram and Hart liaison is indeed guardian of the crooked law firm based in a skyscraper.

Matthias Pavayne

This multiple murderer is the one who's dragging Spike down to hell in early season five. He's been trapped in Wolfram and Hart, which he haunts. His first name (ironically meaning "Gift of God") is old-fashioned to match his eighteenth-century origin. It's a Bible name, one more in Whedon's series of evil religious figures like Caleb and more obviously, the evil doctor who altered River, Dr. Mathias. In "Hell Bound" (A5.4), Pavayne offers Spike his body back in a sort of "deal with the devil" or "gift from God," and Spike refuses in order to save Fred's life. The last name appears made-up, probably a variant on "pain."

Mesekhtet

Mesekhtet (the little girl in the White Room) has an Egyptian name suggesting her ancient nature as well as Wolfram and Hart's worldwide influence. She's meant to be an ancient aide of the god Ra, one of the five Ra-Tet (Mesektet, Manjet, Ashet, Semkhet and Ma'at) who are all targeted in "Long Day's Journey" (A4.9). In the real myths, these were the boats that carried Ra across the heavens.

Nina Ash

Of the (admittedly) many name meanings for Nina across cultures, the Hebrew *God has shown favor* and *friend* in Arabic seem to fit best. Nina the werewolf proves a great friend and blessing to Angel, showing him he can date. Nina Pickering, the werewolf from *Being Human,* may be named for her, as her show brings up the reference.

The ash tree is most known for being the world tree of life and wisdom in Norse myth, a magical tree that held all the world together. A tree of magic, life, and feminine power is a good parallel for Nina. There was a belief that ashwood was incorruptible and could cure wounds, much like a werewolf's quick healing (Watts 17).

Sahjhan

Sahjhan is a chaotic demon who can shift through time and brings Daniel Holtz to the present. His name sounds Arabic, connected as he is with the Nyazian Scrolls and the Resikhian Urn. In fact, Shahjahan is Persian for "king of the world," which makes sense for this controller of time and space.

Skip

The mercenary Skip looks alien and ferocious, but in fact he's quite pleasant, much like Clem. His name, an American nickname for Skipper, captain, is just as casual and friendly. (He takes on the "captain" role while guiding Cordelia to ascension.) Both his name and demeanor are jarring to Angel, who comes in expecting a fight. With his love of movies and cool armor, he's a tribute to Skip Schoolnik, a producer and director for *Buffy* and *Angel,* including "That Vision Thing" (A3.2), which introduced the character.

Doctor Sparrow

Doctor Sparrow performs creepy surgeries for Wolfram and Hart in "Conviction" (A5.1), "Smile Time" (A5.14), and

"Shells" (A5.16). A sparrow is a very urban bird, appearing as harmless as the doctor himself. In Whedon fashion, this doctor is far more than his pleasant name suggests.

Wolfram and Hart

The "Wolf," "Ram" and "Hart," also known as the mysterious "Senior Partners," are a mysterious cabal of ancient demons. The term "senior" puns on their top standing at the law firm and the ancient nature, of course. The name Wolfram and Hart immediately suggests savagery – a wolf preying on a hart or even a heart and tearing it to pieces.

The ram is a symbol of leadership, symbol of Ares, god of war. Wolves are known for ferocity, but also strength in the unity of their pack, much like the law firm itself. The stag or hart was used as a symbol of regeneration, because of the way it renews its antlers. It was prey, often reflecting the sacrificed king, but it would return the next year and the next. The lawyers slaughter Angel and his team as well as each other, but most of those sacrificed return each time, as death is far from permanent. A contract is a contract, after all.

Buffyverse Family Members

Kathy

Young Liam's little sister, named "pure" for her innocence. The show suggests that Kathy's belief that her brother is an angel inspired his new name of "Angelus." Thus Kathy's one permanent mark on the world was to name her immortal brother.

Roger Burkle and Roger Wyndam-Pryce

Roger and Roger are cast as shadows – Wesley's father is callous, dismissive, and apparently abusive, while Fred's is friendly and supportive. One is terribly British, the other terribly Texan. Roger is a manly name meaning "famous with the spear." Wesley's father is a Watcher, while Fred's father seems quite adaptable to combat.

Trish Burkle
Trish, from Patricia, means "noble," and indeed the woman seems noble of spirit if not pedigree. She also shortens her name, making her seem friendly and approachable, much like her daughter Fred.

Lavinia and Sophronia Fairweather
Lavinia Fairweather, also known as Vin, is a witch and Rupert Giles's great aunt. Her first and last name suggest pleasure and delight, as in fact, she and her sister Sophronia pursue hedonistic lives, while perpetually young. "I know what you'd say. That after all these years we're still using people. All we're doing is helping them play the roles they so desperately want," Sophronia comments. They complain that Giles thought their sister Edna, his grandmother, was "so morally superior, just because she got wrinkly and died." Vin means wine in French, the perfect tool for heedless fun, devoid of consequences. Both names are long, flowery and romantic, in contrast with the curt religious name Edna. Their last name, Fairweather, emphasizes their lighthearted dispositions. Both characters were intended for the *Ripper* spinoff, and resemble Anthony Stewart Head's daughters, who might have played them. They appear in the *Angel and Faith* comics.

In *The Aeneid,* Lavinia marries the hero Aeneas and becomes mother of the Roman people. Sophronia is an ancient name meaning wise or judicious. Both names appear to fit the heedless women badly, so it's no surprise they shorten them.

Edna Fairweather Giles
Edna Giles, born Edna Fairweather, appears in the Whedon comic *Tales of the Vampires.* Forced to meet a chained vampire, she insists, "I have a tale I want to hear" and demands his story, not the story of other vampires. She

grows up to become a prominent member of the Watchers Council. Edna is very much the unformed girl, as her name is the Anglicized form of the Irish and Scottish name Eithne, "kernel" in Gaelic. It is also related to Eden, the paradise of youth. With a religious name, Edna is part of the establishment as Watchers' Council, but she's a sympathetic figure who gives young Giles smart advice.

Alonna Gunn
Alonna comes from Alan and means "little rock." Her role as her brother's sense of purpose and support system is made clear when he loses her. Her name is linked with Zoe Alleyne Washburne – perhaps warrior Zoe is a reimagining or continuation of this character – who she might have become if she'd grown up among the gangs of L.A. rather than dying prematurely.

George Patrick Lehane
George means farmer or earthworker, while Patrick is the patron saint of Ireland. This becomes a solid, generic name for Faith's salt-of-the-earth father, nodding also to their Irish roots. He appears in the *Angel and Faith* comic *Daddy Issues*.

Beth Maclay
Tara's "Cousin Beth" is in every way compliant with the patriarchy. As such she's Buffy's opposite, yet their names are linked. Like many linked opposites, like Angel and Spike, they are shadows for each other. Beth is a nickname for Elizabeth, and Buffy most likely is as well. Elizabeth means "Pledged to God," and Beth is certainly compliant with her religious and conformist duties.

Anne Pratt
Spike's mother's name is "Anne," obviously linking her with Buffy (and possibly with Anya, Spike's other relationship). As revealed in the DVD commentary of "Lies My Parents Told Me" (B7.17). Caroline Lagerfelt, who

91

played Spike's mother, was actually chosen due to her potential resemblance to a middle-aged Buffy. As with Spike's relationship with Buffy, the one with his mother is transformative – Buffy inspires him to be a champion, while guilt and despair over his mother's actions drives him to be a murderer once more.

> Spike doted on his original human mother, and in turn she nurtured him and encouraged his pathetic poetics – at least while she was still human. After her conversion to vampire-dom, however, she does not share her son's inherent humanistic leanings. Spike displays the first inkling of his still-evident humanity by turning his mother into a vampire in an attempt to end her sickly human existence and bring her some measure of comfort, but in more typical callous vampire fashion she responds by belittling him, his poetry and his excessive love for her. Then in a perverse twist of this familial love, she attempts to seduce her son, horrifying Spike to such an extent that he is driven to kill her moments after granting her eternal life. (Lowe)

Ira Rosenberg

Ira means "watchful" in Hebrew. His only mention is when Willow notes in "Passion" (B3.17), "Ira Rosenberg's only daughter nailing crucifixes to her bedroom wall? I have to go over to Xander's house just to watch *A Charlie Brown Christmas* every year." Apparently, his only function in the story is to keep a "watch" on her.

Sheila Rosenberg

The meaning of the name Sheila, derived from Cecilia, is "blind." As shown through her single appearance in "Gingerbread" (B3.11), she's terribly blind to everything Willow is. Willow is a talented witch and genius at school, but apparently their last conversation involved *Mr. Rogers*.

Hank Summers

Hank is an American name derived from Henry, "Ruler of an estate." Sadly for Buffy, Hank is no longer her family patriarch, and rarely checks in with her. Far from the leader of his own small kingdom, he runs off to Europe with his secretary and leaves Buffy to defend her home and town without him.

Joyce Summers

Joyce is derived from "Josse," meaning "lord." While she doesn't appear to be the "Joss" character of the story, she is the parent of Buffy, as Joss is parent to the *Buffy* show. Joyce is also considered related to "rejoice." While Joyce is not an excessively bouncy character, she truly loves both her daughters just as they are, and rejoices in their gifts, even, finally, Buffy's slayer powers. As the normal person of the early seasons, who must be kept ignorant of all Buffy does, she represents the ordinary joys of life, going to dances, living in a safe home, all the normalcy Buffy is too often denied.

Nikki Wood

The mother of Robin Wood and a slayer. Nikki, from Nicholas, means "victory of the people," while Nike was the Greek goddess of victory. This is sadly ironic, as she's killed in her first appearance, when she faces Spike. Still as the Slayer, she represented the people's triumph over the world of death and she protected them. She may be named for Nicky Brendon (Xander). Reportedly, Miss Calendar was to be called Nikki, but Nicky Brendon kept getting confused with her. Wood suggests a goddess of nature and the forest as well as a slayer's chosen stake.

Buffyverse Comics Characters

Whedon edited and wrote part of the books *Tales of the Vampires* and *Tales of the Slayers*, following both through history. Likewise he's the producer and occasional writer for the *Buffy* and *Angel* continuation comics. While the early *Buffy* and *Angel* comics are not considered canon, some leeway must be given to the last IDW *Angel* comic *Long Night's Journey,* which Whedon wrote himself.

"Buffy Season Eight" is the 40 episode comic book

series written by Whedon, Espenson, and their team, collected in eight volumes (2007-2011). A five volume season nine followed (2011-2013). The new format allows unlimited special effects as they fight shapeshifters and travel the world. Whedon has declared Season Eight "canon in the Buffy world." As he puts it, "I understand it that way 'cause I'M WRITING IT" ("Joss to Never Learn..."). Accompanying this came *Angel: After the Fall* and *Angel & Faith,* complete with old and new allies and villains.

Aluwyn/Saga Vasuki

This is Willow's lovely snake-bodied mentor (who is a green-skinned woman from the waist up). She's ambiguously moral, as Willow chooses her particularly *because* she's untrustworthy. Her snake attributes emphasize this issue. In English the meaning of the name Elwyn is "wise friend." Vasuki, from India, means king of the serpents. He ruled over the nagas in Hindu legend. As such, both names fit quite well. Saga is probably a variant on the title "sage."

Anaheed and Tumble

This pair are Buffy's roommates introduced in the first season nine comic, and thus created by Whedon.

Anaheed, who finished college with a graduate degree and an attempt to write the great American novel, is a fact checker online. As revealed eventually, she's a secret slayer keeping an eye on Buffy. In Armenian, Anahid is a "moon goddess," hinting at her supernatural status. She's a chaste figure like Diana (even though Anaheed appears bi) and silent watcher over the world.

Tumble is more the clichéd slacker, who's interested in starting a band with Spike. During their housewarming party, Dawn guesses that tumble is short for "rough and" "-weed" or " - dry." He tells her she's wrong each time, but offers no other information. His name seems like "Oz," an unusual, rule-breaking choice that sounds a bit better than "drifter." Like Oz, he's taciturn, musically-inclined, and unambitious.

Betta George

Betta George is a giant floating telepathic fish known as a Splenden Beast. He first appears in the Mosaic Wellness Center, in *Spike: Asylum*. Later, Betta George participates in the Fall of Los Angeles, as he's kidnapped by Gunn, and finally joins Angel's team after the year is reversed.

Betta is an unusual variant on Elizabeth, as Buffy is, while George is a very common male first name. Having one female name and one male emphasizes his liminal status (as does being a telepathic floating fish). George means farmer or earthworker, stressing his humble position. Comics writer Brian Lynch says in *Angel: After the Fall*, that Betta George is an audience surrogate. "He's supposed to be the most normal character. Because I know that if you have a talking fish hanging out with everyone's favorite characters, people are going to not like him immediately. Because he could be Jar Jar very easily. So I try to make him the nicest, most normal character, and the one who would react like the audience would react."

Bugs

In *Buffy the Vampire Slayer Season 9: Magical Mystery Tour Featuring the Beatles* (reprinted in *Freefall*, B9.1), Spike gives each bug crew member of his spaceship an earth name (Paolo, Elizabeth, Frisky, Bub, Lester, Jumpy, Fido, Irene, Spotty and Rick). Though the bugs feel honored, Spike's names are meant as pet names (Frisky, Fido) or otherwise dehumanizing (Jumpy, Spotty) in many cases. There's a possibility Elizabeth the bug is named for Buffy. Irene means "peace," but she unfortunately turns into a mindless predator as the first vampire bug.

Cordelia the Dragon

Angel tames the dragon seen at the end of "Not Fade Away" (A5.22) in the *Angel: After the Fall* comics. Angel later reveals that he had jumped off a building and critically injured himself, but the dragon carried him to Wolfram and Hart to recover. As Angel says:

> It still took months to heal. Every second of that time was spent awake, and the pain….I'm not a stranger to pain but this, this was mind-numbing. To get through it without snapping I learned to focus on something else. I imagined you [Cordelia]. I talked to you the entire time. I didn't actively choose you. When I'm conscious it still hurts to say your name. But when I needed someone, there you were. I guess it makes sense, during my time in L.A you were what kept me sane. The dragon guarded me night and day. Heard every rant, every one-sided conversation. And he thought I was talking to him. He thinks his name is your name. Is that weird? (*Angel: After the Fall 3*)

Though the dragon is more of a pet than a person, it represents help from above, a power beyond what Angel himself can bring to the fight. Thus the dragon becomes Angel's new Cordelia, though he's far less of an emotional support, a pale shadow of the original.

When the Groosalugg arrives on the scene, he is riding a flying horse he's also named Cordelia (it is a less impressive imitation of Angel's dragon, just as Groo's romance with Cordelia was less epic and impactful than Angel's with her). After L.A. is saved, Groo inherits the dragon to go on grandiose medieval rescues. As he notes, this way Cordelia will always be with him with "two Cordy's" of his own, pegasus and dragon. Though unlucky in love, he remains a champion of earth.

Dez

Angel teams up with a werepanther named Desdemona (Dez for short) in the comic *Angel: Aftermath*. As she says of herself, "Do I look like a jaguar? Act like one? Talk like one? Yes, I was born that way, but I don't remember it. As far as I'm concerned, I'm a person who can shift into a cat. I'm fully assimilated..." Many "fully assimilated" foreigners shorten their names thus to better fit in, and indeed, Dez hides her magical abilities behind the look of normalcy. Her nickname also suggests reckless toughness.

Her full name, from *Othello,* suggests she'll betray Angel and his friends, but in fact, Desdemona was *falsely* believed to be unfaithful. While Dez has secrets and appears to be casting spells on humans to transform them into helpless animals, she's actually on the side of good.

Genevieve Savidge

This slayer-turned-bad is an aristocrat who insists, "Buffy has forced our kind to be the serfs of this world, when we should have been lording over the masses" (*No Future for You,* B8.2). Faith is sent to take her down. While Genevieve is a stately French name meaning "white wave," it also has power. Saint Genevieve, patron saint of Paris, was believed to have protected her city from Attila the Hun. She goes by the friendlier "Gigi" when not trading on her lordly identity. Her last name is clearly a play on "savage."

Jamaerah/Myresto "Myr" Mor

> ANNE: You're an angel for helping out the way you have.
> JAMES: Well, not exactly.

Jamaerah or "James" joins Angel Investigations after the Fall of L.A. and the team's recovery. There's irony in hosting an actual angel, whose goodness must call Angel's into question. He's an agent of the Powers that Be and a Potentiate, a warrior-angel who sees visions of the future and kills people for crimes that they *would* commit, until Angel convinces them to stop. James means "he who supplants," likewise emphasizing his possible usurping of the real Angel's position. In angel lore, Jamaerah is an angel of manifestation, who aids people to achieve their heart's desires.

After a few books pass, Jamaerah reveals himself as the demon Myresto "Myr" Mor, who plans to turn the earth into a demonic breeding farm. He is indeed a guide to achieving possibilities...the murderous kind. He notes,

"When I first came here, I saw the potential. I saw a raw world swarming with millions of hosts just waiting to be filled. To be... evolved. [...] The death and rebirth of this world will be hailed for ages to come." His demon name, Myresto "Myr" Mor, seems related to myriad and more, suggesting his need to fill the earth with demonkind.

Laura Kay Weathermill and Polyphemus

In *Angel: Immortality For Dummies,* former watcher Laura Kay Weathermill joins Angel's team, along with her Monasterenser Magnaserm (a sentient floating encyclopedia) named Polyphemus. He's clearly named after the Cyclops from *The Odyssey,* while Monasterenser Magnaserm sounds like a bestiary or medieval grimmoire. As such, they're linked with the ancient classics. Laura comes from the laurel tree, for triumph, while her other names make her sound particularly British.

Perfect Jheung and Galahad

Perfect Jheung, a vampire from Angel's past, appears in the Angel comic *Long Night's Journey.* He insists Angel's ensoulment was a test to see if such a thing could be accomplished. "When you proved successful, you were followed, examined, studied. All the while, your successor being searched for. The one to which the curse would grant great power and salvation. Turn into the perfect champion...me." However, his ensoulment didn't work, and he demands Angel tell him why.

"Jheung" may come from the word "Righteous," a fitting name, as he believes he is meant to be the vampire with a soul, not Angel. His addition of the word "perfect" emphasizes self-naming and arrogance – he truly believes himself a perfect person. "For someone who's perfect, you whine a lot," Angel says, deflating him before beating him.

Galahad, as they call the demon knight under Perfect Jheung's control, is pure champion, like his Arthurian namesake. However, like the warriors of Pylea and medieval Galahad himself, he has an absolute view of justice. There is none of the flexibility and compassion that define Angel and prove why Angel deserves his soul.

Robert Dowling

This SFPD officer is a regular in *Buffy the Vampire Slayer Season Nine*. Much like Kate Lockley, he's a police officer who wants to end the vampire menace. Robert means "bright fame," and he's certainly looking to make a name for himself. Dowling is one letter off from Downing, where the British Prime Minister works, suggesting government and law. It's related to the Old English for "darling," and in fact, he and Buffy begin to date.

Roche and Sophie Downs

Young Edna Fairweather, soon to be Edna Giles and the grandmother of Rupert, is sent to meet the chained-up vampire Roche in *Tales of the Vampires*. "Why would a vampire as powerful as Roche claims to be allow himself to be used for children's story hour?" she asks perceptively.

The name Roche is French, from the Latin word for rock. He is of course stone-hearted and imprisoned in a stone dungeon underground. The name makes him sound like something of a cockroach, and also emphasizes his French origin.

Names feature significantly in his tale: Edna calls him on his storytelling after he describes being turned. "We study languages, you halfwit. 'Die Eingame.' The lovely, in the feminine. Not a man as you unconvincingly claimed but a woman." In fact, the frightening vampire's sire is Sophie Downs, the little girl with blonde sausage curls. Everything about her name suggests a commonplaceness – Sophie is an ordinary girl's name, and Downs suggests humility. Of course, Sophie means wisdom, hinting at her longevity, and Downs suggests the down-low, a hidden agenda.

Satsu

Satsu first appears in the season eight comics, where she surprised fans by embarking on a brief lesbian affair with

Buffy. "Satsu" is a Japanese word (殺) meaning "murder" or "kill," so the name actually can be translated as "Slayer." Assuming she didn't give herself this name as Angel or Spike did upon discovering her new powers, this could suggest Satsu was destined to become the slayer. It could also be a short form of the given name *Satsuki* (the month of May), suggesting springtime, renewal and new growth in the relationship she brings to Buffy.

Severin/The Siphon
A mysterious young vampire hunter, Severin can drain the mystical energy from whomever he touches, giving him his superhero nickname. "You don't deserve the power you have so I'm going to take it," he tells Buffy. Severin sounds "severe," with connotations of cruel Professor Severus Snape from *Harry Potter*.

Simone Doffler
Simone is one of Buffy's new slayer army in the season eight comics, until she decides slayers are superior to normal people and rebels against Buffy's orders. "They wanted us to live under their rules, now we can make them live under ours. We can bring our oppressors to their knees. We can be the agents of change and fear we were meant to be. It's who we are," she insists.

As discussed in the *Firefly* section, Simon was the name of several disciples of Jesus, but also of great revolutionaries like Simon Maccabeus. Simone begins as a disciple of Buffy, but quickly switches allegiance. Simon comes from Hebrew meaning "He who has heard/hears [the word of God]," while Simon, the son of Jacob, commits a great act of violence and betrays his family. Simone, inspired by her own conscience not by Buffy's rules, makes herself a "slaypire," betraying all Buffy stands for.

The surname "Doffler" or "Doppler" comes from the Low German "Dabel," a nickname for a gambler, or from an occupational name for a maker of dice, from "dopel," die. Simone is certainly a gambler as she rebels against Buffy's regime and the new slayer order. The name is also related to Doppelganger, one's shadow-double, which Simone is for Buffy. As Buffy must be the voice of rules and responsibility, Simone voices her own secret fantasies that Slayers are all-powerful and have a right to rule the world.

Twilight

The "Big Bad" of the season eight comics is a flying masked figure called Twilight. While it sounds ominous with a philosophy of the sun setting on the world of magic, it has an unfortunate connotation. "My God, is that really the name you picked? Twilight? Y'know I lived that idea first, right?" Buffy asks, referencing the popular teen series about a girl in a vampire love triangle (*Twilight*, B8.7). In the *Spike* comic, Spike says, "Good to see you dropped the Twilight act. I hear the chick who writes the gothic novels is litigious."

Firefly

In a dystopian future, a team of ragtag salvagers and thieves get into colorful adventures at the frontier's edge. All the *Firefly* characters have nameflips of some sort, designed to defy expectations. Kaywinnit and Malcolm shorten theirs. Hoban Washburne uses his last name. Derrial Book uses an alias. Jayne is a girl's name. Simon and River have a Chinese last name, and if Kaylee had been Chinese as intended, she would have had a British one. Inara, though she acts like a geisha, is named for a Hittite goddess of the land. Zoe's name is Greek for Eve – both myth names come from the least likely of origins.

Firefly Main Characters

Shepherd Derrial Book/Henry Evans

Having a preacher named Shepherd Book is practically too perfect for words (no pun intended). In fact, it is *too* perfect – that's not the name he was born with.

Shepherd Book was born as the more prosaic Henry Evans, According to the comic, *The Shepherd's Tale*, he grew up in the bad part of town with an abusive father, and then renamed himself...by murdering Alliance cadet Derrial Book and stealing his name. He thus infiltrated the military on a mission for the independents.

Certainly, Book sounds like a name he took on, as popes and nuns change their names to suggest a new holy calling. However, it appears Book was merely the surname of another man. Even before turning religious, the Shepherd felt drawn to books and the name behind them.

103

He uses the word "book" to thus fictionalize his life. Wilcox calls Book "A man whose name is all about telling the right story" ("I Don't Hold to That" 163).

The name Derrial is Whedon's adaptation of Darryl, which is French for the surname d'Airelle, someone from the town of Airelle. The town in turn is derived from the word for "open spaces." So Derrial Book is from the land of open spaces, the frontier, as well as being a man of the book. In a world of characters choosing their own names, as Angel, Spike, and others do, this is far more appropriate than dull Henry Evans.

Hoban "Wash" Washburne

This character is only ever referred to as "Wash," the first syllable of his surname. When Mal confronts him in the *Serenity* film novelization, Wash explains, "Why would anyone call themselves Hoban?" (250).

"Hoban" is an Irish surname, meaning "son of Ubain," with the "ban" in "Ubain" meaning white in Gaelic (SurnameDB). Wash is blond, but also awkwardly named to honor (most likely) a family surname which in itself honors a distant ancestor. It's a name designed to pay homage to others, so it's no surprise he throws it off.

"Washburne" comes from the Saxon for "from the flooding brook," with "wash" meaning "swift moving current of a stream," and "burn" referring to a brook or a small stream. As he travels with the flow like "a leaf on the wind," this seems to be a strong metaphor for the character.

Calling a pilot a washout is an insult of course. This is likely an ironic name, as Wash is quite skilled as a pilot, if rather juvenile. However, Wash as a name is considered a nickname for "Washington," the rebel leader who founded the United States. Thus the simple syllable contains more gravitas than first appears.

During the commentary on "War Stories" (F1.10), Tudyk notes that he believes Wash served in the Unification War as a pilot (though for which side is unclear). His name, of course, suggests the rebel side, as does his closeness with Zoe and Mal. Tudyk also jokes that Wash's ship was shot down on its first flight and he was put in a POW camp, where he spent the remainder of the war entertaining the other prisoners with shadow puppets.

Inara Serra

Inara was an obscure Hittite goddess over the land and beasts (a Demeter rather than precisely an Aphrodite figure). In "The Anatolian Myth of Illuyanka," nearly the only account left of her, she provided lavish food and drink for the gods, lulling the enemy serpents into a stupor. Then she went and beguiled the mortal hero Hupasiya, saying that he should come with her. Though he had a wife and children, he replied, "If I may sleep with you, then I will come and perform your heart's desire." She agreed. With his aid, she slew an enemy serpent. Then she took him to her magnificent home and warned him that if he looked out the window for her he would never return to his family. When he broke the taboo, she was forced to kill him (Beckman).

Inara travels with Mal, not the reverse, but certainly he longs to sleep with her. Together they slay their enemies and win the day on several occasions. It's possible that if the story had progressed, Mal would have broken her taboo and been harmed...as it is, he crosses an emotional barrier with her and she decides to leave in "Heart of Gold" (F1.13).

She's certainly a goddess figure on the ship, the essence of femininity and all the feminine culture: art, refinement, sophistication of dress and manner. She's a guide to femininity for the other characters: She doesn't just train Mal in proper behavior but does Kaylee's hair, cares for River, and exists at the opposite end of the spectrum from Zoe.

When she encounters the incredibly feminine Saffron, complete with her all-too-practiced vulnerability, Inara is instantly suspicious. She understands everything about Saffron because they're two of a kind, though Inara is presented as the "good one" and Saffron as the "bad one." In "Trash" (F1.11), Saffron outwits Mal once more, and Inara must save the day along with the naked captain. While it's been used occasionally since the 1990s, Inara's use is a name grew significantly as a result of the television show (appellationmountain).

Her last name sounds like the female name Sarah, princess, or Serene. Two "first names" makes her sound particularly approachable and feminine. The first and last names pair well together, with a musical quality. Serra is actually Italian for mountains, much like the American Sierras. Once more, she is a goddess of the land, who nonetheless travels to great heights with Mal.

Jayne Cobb

> RIVER: Jayne is a girl's name.
> JAYNE: Well, Jayne ain't a girl. (to Simon) She starts in on that "girl's name" thing, I'll show her good an' all I got man parts. ("Trash," F1.11)

"I'd never been asked to play a girl before, so I knew I'd need to summon my inner hero, Carol Burnett," Adam Baldwin jokes in his forward to *Better Days and Other Stories.* Like ambiguously named Angel, Fred, Lindsey, Mal and Zoe's old war buddy Tracey Smith, and so forth, Jayne has a gender-swapped name. This is ironic as he is the most classically male character on *Firefly.* He's aggressive, brutish, crude, and callous. His one great love appears to be his gun collection. Some fans see a connection with "A Boy Named Sue," the Johnny Cash song about a boy who's so-named to toughen him up. If this is true in Jayne's case, it certainly worked. He notes in the *Serenity* film: "I'll kill a man in a fair fight...or if I think he's gonna start a fair fight, or if he bothers me, or if there's a woman, or I'm gettin' paid – mostly only when I'm gettin' paid." Adam Baldwin considers Jayne "the practical guy, a hands-on problem

106

solver" (*Firefly: The Official Companion* I:94). "It's like 'Cut to the chase, guys! Quit your pussyfooting around and all your existential musings about the goodness of this existence. Let's go kill them!" (*Firefly: The Official Companion* I:94).

By giving him nuance with the name Jayne, as with the surprising events of "Jaynestown" (F1.7), Whedon appears to be offering Jayne more breadth – he is more than he appears at first glance, with the potential to grow still further. Baldwin adds, "Joss's way with words provided me the opportunity to play a tough guy (girl's name) with comedic flavor" (*Better Days*).

Lastly and most logically, Jayne's name also appears a portmanteau or squashing-together of John Wayne (Wilcox and Cochran, "Introduction" 5). Of course, it's not always a girl's name: It is derived from the English surname Jayne from Worcester, so it is often used as a family name, or male first name from the family surname. As such, it's a patronym of Jan, which comes from John. He was an apostle, thus an assistant, if Mal or River is the Christ figure of the story. It's also the most common male name and thus an emblem of Jayne's maleness, ironically hidden under a "girl's name." Cobb fits the character well as it's Anglo-Saxon for a "very large man" or one of impressive features and great strength.

When the crew become ambulance staff in "Ariel" (F1.9), they all have fake badge names, viewable up close in *Firefly: The Official Visual Companion* II (67). Mal's fake name is Miles, which means "Soldier" in the Latin. However, his last name, Arixoen, has a dirty sound to it. Wash's "Beauma Sclevages" and Zoe's "Q. Kumamota" are likewise suspicious. Jayne, labeled with the hysterically funny "girl's name" of Kiki LaRue may actually be the cleanest.

Kaywinnit Lee "Kaylee" Frye

Kaywinnit is a whimsical exotic name. With all its syllables, it appears a name for an elegant lady. In fact, the entire name appears when she enters the ball in "Shindig" (F1.4) for her Cinderella or *Gone with the Wind* moment. (Mal even describes her as "crying Cinderella tears.") She is elegant and confident as well as excited, and she's soon charmed all the men just by being herself – clever, mechanical, eager, and pretty. As her actress notes:

> Everyone trusts Kaylee, and she's easy to identify with. People find her warm. I've heard her described as the heart of the ship. She loves that life. She loves being on that ship. She loves all of those people. And she's the only one who loves all of them incredibly genuinely. (Staite)

In the Whedonesque tradition of self-naming, she calls herself the diminutive Kaylee – it's as short, sweet, and endearing as she is. "You manage to find the bright side to every single thing," Simon tells her in "The Message" (F1.12). Everyone, from taciturn Jayne to grouchy Mal, loves her.

In English, Kaylee is sometimes a hyphenate of Kay (a British short form of Katherine, Greek for "pure") and Lee (meaning meadow): She becomes one more of Whedon's nature goddesses. The name is also an American variant on Kayla, Arabic and Hebrew for "laurel" or "crown." In Irish a céilidh (pronounced kaylee) is a celebration or dance party. Thus she's a pure figure of celebration and merriment, sparkling under a victory crown, a name which certainly fits, though it is River not Kaylee who's seen dancing in a meadow.

She may be an homage to *X-Men*'s Kitty Pryde as Buffy was – though she's tiny, sweet, and innocent-looking, Kaylee is certainly capable of caring for herself and saves the day on many occasions. Despite her charm, she's unquestioningly a competent member of the team. Whedon's mother, Lee Stearns, may be another parallel.

The surname Frye is British, from the Old English "freo" or "frig" meaning "free (born)" or from the Middle English/French, meaning "small." Frye may also be a pun on "smallfry," nodding to her tiny size. Mal and Jayne call her "Little Kaylee" on occasion, and characters often call her Mei-mei, a nickname used for "little sister" in Chinese. Tiny and completely free to sail with Mal or quit, form relationships, do as she wishes in the safety of Serenity, both names fit her perfectly.

Malcolm "Mal" Reynolds

Everybody calls Malcolm Reynolds "Mal." River points out that in the Latin, Mal means "Bad." He certainly prides himself on being the bad boy with his iconic line, "I aim to misbehave." Malcolm means "devotee of St. Colomba" – This saint preached to and converted much of Scotland. Captain Mal used to be called Malcolm, and in fact, used to wear a cross. However, he has turned his back on this life after the Battle of Serenity Valley, and simply goes by Mal. At the same time, he has a deep moral code and fights for the innocents who cannot defend themselves

Malcolm Reynolds appears to be a Robin Hood figure, the son of a wealthy rancher, who should have become a powerful ruler. However, he found himself rebelling against the establishment after he lost everything. Thus he transformed into leader of a tiny band fleeing the law and living as they wish (not to mention robbing the rich to feed and medicate the poor). Malcolm was a name given to four Scottish kings, including Malcolm, Prince of Cumberland, in Shakespeare's *Macbeth*. Their history with England is filled with war and uprisings, echoing Malcolm Reynolds' own path. Malcolm X is another defiant namesake.

The ancient family motto for Reynolds was *Jus meum tuebor*, "I will defend my right" (SurnameDB). Malcolm Reynolds often fights to defend his small kingdom – his ship and those on it. Reynolds is a patronymic surname meaning "son of Reynold." Reynold itself means "powerful ruler" from "rey," king, and "wald," strong. The English Reynolds were a well-established family of lords, who arrived in England with the Norman Conquest of 1066. They ruled in Somerset and in the 12th century, spread to

Scotland and Ireland. Mal is ruler of his ship and also the son of a wealthy rancher – he's just a king is exile.

The most ancient Reynolds Coat of Arms was a silver shield with a portcullis and three blue bars and a fox crest. His last name of course sounds like Reynard, the anthropomorphic red fox and trickster figure out of Western European folklore. The fox is known through fiction for his tricky thievery and cleverness, as he escapes traps laid by the establishment each time.

River Tam
A river is beautiful and natural, constantly in motion much as River herself is. "The river is not a 'body' of water but a stream: with its flow and its floodings, it functions not statically, but dynamically, and it becomes the basis for the historical reckoning of time itself" (Biedermann 285). Rivers could be benign and violent in turn, nourishing fields, or sweeping away villagers. They also emphasized change.

"The symbolism of rivers and running water is simultaneously that of 'universal potentiality' and that of 'the fluidity of forms' of fertility, death, and renewal" (Chevalier and Gheerbrant 808). The great cosmic river represents the lifecycle as all beings are pulled into it, interconnected through the world. River began as total potential, before the government abused her. Now, her potential is even greater, as she has the power to read minds and understand far more than ever.

In books, rivers often represent a type of inherent magic. Water symbolizes the feminine: "Because river-water sustains life, many river gods represent fertility and prosperity" (Shepherd 34). In India, rivers are the veins of Mother Earth. Ships in many cultures were linked with water deities. Serenity is admittedly a spaceship, but River bonds with it, becoming goddess of the ship and all within.

Of course, River is not natural at all – she is a hybrid built by the Alliance doctors. As such, she's linked with the Reavers whose secrets are buried in her mind. "The facts

110

that 'River' and 'Reaver' sound so much alike and that they are both products of government experimentation that resulted in, respectively, a purposeful and an accidental increase in violence and aggression—suggests their function as analogues" (Buckman 181). In the end, she is the Reavers' nemesis, the only one who can defeat them.

Though also a Scottish hat, Tam is most likely related to the Chinese last name Tan, named for the state. It seems Simon and River's family is partly Chinese, or named for them, even if the characters don't appear Asian.

Serenity

The spacecraft, named for the Battle of Serenity Valley, is often called the show's tenth character. In the film, the Operative notes that Serenity Valley was anything but. It was the "Bloodiest battle of the entire war. The Independents held the valley for seven weeks, two of them after their high command had surrendered. 68% casualty rate" (*Serenity*).

The ship Serenity itself may hint at the Serenity prayer, which is a motto for choosing one's battles.

> God, give me grace to accept with serenity
> the things that cannot be changed,
> Courage to change the things
> which should be changed,
> and the Wisdom to distinguish
> the one from the other.
> Living one day at a time,
> Enjoying one moment at a time,
> Accepting hardship as a pathway to peace,
> Taking, as Jesus did,
> This sinful world as it is,
> Not as I would have it,
> Trusting that You will make all things right,
> If I surrender to Your will,
> So that I may be reasonably happy in this life,
> And supremely happy with You forever in the next.
> Amen.

Frequently just the first six lines are used. Certainly, life on

Serenity involves a constant battle between the sinful world and the struggle to survive, faith and practicality (as embodied by Book and Jayne, both advisors to the torn Captain Mal). As they get into scrapes and persevere through them, one day at a time, they struggle to find the "serenity" they are carried within.

Simon Tam

Simon is the most ordinary name on the ship, and indeed, he seems too stuffy and buttoned up for a nickname. His name emphasizes that he's not from the frontier but from a civilized world viewers would recognize. Indeed the flashback to his childhood shows action figures, requests for a cellphone upgrade, homework, and an otherwise prosaic life. As such, he's the most like a contemporary American, the outsider and our guide to life on the ship. He may be named for the musician Simon Tam (born March 30, 1981) who founded the Asian American dance-rock band, The Slants.

Simon comes from Hebrew meaning "He who has heard/hears [the word of God]." Simon the zealot was one of Jesus's apostles, as was Peter, who was originally called Simon. Both men left everything in their previous lives to follow Jesus. If River is the Chosen One, who brings the truth that will convert the world in *Serenity*, then Simon takes his place as the most important of her disciples. At Jesus's side, Peter witnessed great miracles as Jesus raised Jairus's daughter from the dead (Mark 5:35-43). Simon Tam witnesses the innocent River's similar rise from suspended animation.

The Old Testament's Simeon was the son of Jacob, who ignored his father's wishes to slaughter the men who had raped or seduced his sister Dinah. Simon certainly is capable of avenging his sister with violence, and he has already defied his father to rescue and avenge her. In the Bible, Jacob curses Simeon and his brother for their warmongering, and prophecizes that their descendants will be scattered:

112

> Simeon and Levi are brothers – their swords are
> weapons of violence. Let me not enter their council, let
> me not join their assembly, for they have killed men in
> their anger ... Cursed be their anger, so fierce, and their
> fury, so cruel! I will scatter them in Jacob and disperse
> them in Israel. (Gen. 49: 5-7)

Certainly, Simon and River Tam have already vanished into space, parted from their family for perhaps forever.

Simon Maccabeus near the end of the Old Testament was a rebel, who took command of the Maccabees after his brother's capture. They won, and the Hasmonean Dynasty was founded by a resolution at a large assembly "of the priests and the people and of the elders of the land, to the effect that Simon should be their leader and high priest forever, until there should arise a faithful prophet" (1 Maccabees 14:41).

If the series had gone on, Simon may have denied River, as Peter did to Jesus. He may have been martyred for her as Simon Peter and Simon the Zealot were. He may have committed violence to avenge her. Simon may have also joined the new rebellion after Mal's capture and become its leader.

Zoe Alleyne Washburne

Zoe, meaning "life," is an ancient name, a Greek translation of Eve. It appears as far back as the classical period, and was popular with the early Christians, who bestowed it with hopes of eternal life. Only in the nineteenth century did the English-speaking world adopt it.

Seeing Zoe as Eve creates various tracks of symbolism. Zoe is the one to keep Wash on the ship, as he complains in "War Stories" (F1.10) and *Those Left Behind.* However, in many ways she seems the opposite of the famed naked seductress – she loathes Saffron who is more literally an Eve character. Her name may be subtly siding with those who see Eve as an ancestral mother and matriarch rather than a hapless victim. For indeed, Zoe is the matriarch of the ship, ruling it with steadiness when Mal is away or requires her counsel. Jane Espenson notes that Mal and Zoe echo the ship's parents as well as *Firefly's* producers: "The Joss-as-Mal, co-executive producer Marti Noxon as Zoe parallel struck all of us in those days" (1). Whedon similarly explains that Zoe represents Mal's hidden heroism "his honor and the fact that he was such a good leader that this person who is happily married and completely at peace with herself would still follow him into these serious and sometimes dumb situations" (*Serenity Visual Companion* 11). As such, she's the Eve to Mal's Adam, the perfect helpmeet and complement.

Saint Zoe of Rome has a few parallels with the character, thanks to her devotion to St. Peter. She was killed while praying by his tomb. Like Zoe Washburne, she fell victim to the establishment, against whom she rebelled. Zoe was also a Byzantine empress, co-ruler beside her sister Theodora in 1042 and a strong and aggressive ruler for her people.

Alleyne is of Celtic origin, derived from the first name Alan, from the Gaelic "ailin," little rock. With a man's name as surname, and one that means rock, Zoe's militaristic toughness appears once again.

Firefly and Serenity Guest Characters

Adelai Niska

This Czech-speaking leader of a crime syndicate threatens and finally tortures Mal on one memorable occasion. Adelai is the Eastern European variant on Adelaide, meaning "noble." While Niska is the leader, he's far more brutal than his name indicates. The surname is very obscure, appearing more often as a woman's name of uncertain meaning. Thus both names are actually feminine. Like Jayne, the most powerful brute is named for a female, emphasizing the flexibility and unpredictability of the apocalyptic future. His "associates" are Viktor and Crow, though Mal shoves Crow into the engine. With a crow's tattoo covering half his face, he appears to come from a

British/Celtic tradition. There, crows were unlucky birds of death. Viktor means conqueror, and he survives longer.

Atherton Wing

Atherton is a somewhat pretentious, unusual boy's name from a British place, suggesting his family connections and lordly pedigree. It appears more common as a surname, again, suggesting haughty distance. (Sir Warwick Harrow, also at the ball of "Shindig," F1.4, has similar name associations). By contrast, the surname Wing is adventurous and sprightly, though also hinting at his rash temper. He challenges Mal to a duel for Inara in "Shindig."

Badger

Badger sounds more like a code name than a legal one – badgers are known for tenacity and often an annoying quality, as "to badger" means to harass. Badger, who refers to himself as a "businessman," gets Mal into several problematic business situations. Known for his bowler and British accent, he's folksy and approachable. Badgers are fiercely independent and can be fierce fighters, though they appear harmlessly small, much like Badger himself.

Bea

Bea, the leader of the New Resistance, joins the crew in the comic *Serenity: Leaves on the Wind.* Like Kaylee, Wash, and Mal, she shortens her name (from the elegant Beatrice, "she who brings happiness"). She intends to guide Mal like Dante's Beatrice, though she may also bring happiness to the adoring Jayne, verbally sparring with him like her namesake in *Much Ado About Nothing.*

Bester

Bester, the mechanic Kaylee replaces, is probably named for science fiction writer Alfred Bester (a *Babylon 5* character was named for him as well). His *The Demolished Man* is a police procedural that takes place in a future in which mind reading is bought and sold, often used for immoral purposes. *The Stars My Destination* shows a dark future of megacorporations as powerful as governments and cybernetic body enhancement. Many of these elements appear in the *Firefly* universe and may have inspired it.

Fanty and Mingo

Fanty and Mingo give Mal the bank job that goes horribly wrong in *Serenity*, with a Reaver attack. They are named for characters who work for a crime boss in *The Big Combo*. Certainly, their names seem appropriate for frontier goons, shortened to nicknames like Mal and Wash. At the same time, their "cutesy" sound reinforces their lack of skills. In the *Serenity* film novelization, the operative identifies the two goons by their full names: "Mr. Mingojerry Rample. Mr. Fantastic Rample. Twins, born to Alanna Rample and an unknown father. One boy derives his name from a misremembered T.S. Elliot poem, the other from Alanna Rample's expression upon realizing she had a second bun in the oven. A thoroughly unimaginative woman, who passed that trait onto her sons" (170). Fantastic is something of a Puritan frontier name like Patience or Radiance, albeit a silly, exaggerated one.

T.S. Elliot wrote *Old Possum's Book of Practical Cats,* from which the musical *Cats* was adapted. The poem "Mungojerrie and Rumpelteazer" describes a pair of troublemaking cats, who make appropriate namesakes for the *Serenity* pair. If the novel description comes from a cut Whedon moment, rather than the book author's imagination, it marks the appearance of yet another "Alan" or rather "Alanna."

Jubal Early

Jubal Early, the bounty hunter from "Objects in Space" (F1.14) is named for Confederate Civil War General Jubal Anderson Early, an ancestor of Nathan Fillion. Joss Whedon mentions in his DVD commentary that Jubal Early was partly inspired by the *Star Wars* character Boba Fett.

Early was not just a Confederate general, but he is

"credited with being one of the architects of the Lost Cause, the belief by some in the South that the Confederacy had not lost the war, but rather had simply been overwhelmed by the Union's greater numbers" (Lerner 189). As such, he's actually a close parallel for Mal himself.

"Jubal" means stream in Hebrew, making him the perfect nemesis for the Serenity crew, until he is defeated by the greater power, the River. Jubal is a Bible name, one in a list of genealogies who "was the father of all who play stringed instruments and pipes" (Genesis 4:21). Thus he is a musician to River's dancer as he hopes to control her (and in fact make the entire crew "dance to his tune" before she turns the tables on him). Bible names and Western names like "Early" are common in *Firefly* – the former are found on the frontier, while the latter belong more to the establishment. Thus Jubal Early is a blend of both, rogue and government employee. His name is also a warning – he is indeed "early," the first bounty hunter to arrive for River, but not the last.

Dr. Mathias

Dr. Mathias heads the team that alters and experiments on River. (He is mentioned in the *R. Tam Sessions*, and is seen, but not named, in the film *Serenity*, although he is named in the shooting script and novelization.). In the novelization, his first name is given as Philbert (63).

Ironically, the surname means "Gift of God." As an apostle, Mathias replaced Judas, after the latter betrayed Jesus. Robert Matthews, a famed false prophet who led a cult, gave himself this name as well. Thus the name is synonymous with religion, but not goodness. It echoes of religious sanctimoniousness as he calls River a "creature" and dismisses the side effects and suffering she undergoes. Dr. Mathias, like many other religiously-named Whedon characters, is in service to the brutal government. He is finally murdered by the equally sanctimonious Operative.

The Operative
The Operative, an agent of the Alliance government, has no other name or even rank provided. As such, his black ops connection is intensified. He also loses sympathy with his menacing namelessness. This naming also emphasizes his selflessness, as he operates on behalf of others. He tells everyone, "We're making a better world," justifying his murders and atrocities. But as he adds, "I'm not going to live there. How could you think – there's no place for me there, any more than there is for you. Malcolm, I'm a monster. What I do is evil, I've no illusions about it. But it must be done" (*Serenity*). Mal proves that his need to create a "world without sin" in fact created the Reavers. Immoral acts will not redeem the world.

Patience
Ironically, Patience (who threatens Mal in the pilot) has no Patience. However, she has a Puritan name, suitable for those on the frontier. Patience is also used as a Frontier/Redneck name in *Cabin in the Woods*. There's a briefly seen character called Patience in Angel's "Peace Out" (A4.21).

Professor Rao
Rao is the name of River's teacher at the school of her *Serenity* flashback who says, "River, we're not telling people what to think. We're just trying to show them how." Of course, she's proved tragically wrong. "Rao," like "Raja," indicates kingliness in India, and thus establishes the teacher as part of the establishment. The name means "abundance" in Chinese, emphasizing her life as one of the wealthy elite. Interestingly, her name links her with Professor Kavita Rao of Whedon's *X-Men* run, another Indian woman whose beliefs and science threaten the lives of the underdog protagonists.

Reavers

The English word means to rob, spoil, and smash, from the root of "to break." Their name sounds like frontier slang, as no one knows their origin (until the *Serenity* movie). Their philosophy is also unknown – they are only named for their actions, suggesting wildness incarnate, the untamed frontier.

Saffron/Bridget/Yolanda

"So, are you enjoying your own nubile little slave girl?" Zoe asks Mal after he is told he's unwittingly married the helpless, childlike Saffron in "Our Mrs. Reynolds" (F1.6). "Saffron appears eager to serve as dependent helpmeet to Mal and assumes the pose of submissive femininity" (Beadling 57). Of course, he and most of his crew are fooled by her innocence, until she drugs them and steals a shuttle. Her actress, Christina Hendricks describes her, saying, "I decided that Saffron is so good at what she does, and she does it so often, that she has to almost convince herself. So I never tried to play the secret – I just tried to play what was happening at that moment because I think *she* believes it" (*Firefly: The Official Visual Companion* I:165).

The herb saffron goes back to the Biblical "Song of Solomon" (poems of seduction). In the ancient world, prostitutes wore yellow robes, through an association with Eos, the dawn goddess of Greece and her saffron robes (Watts 336). In the Aztec court, the plant was considered an aphrodisiac. The plant was also used as a cheaper substitute for dying cloth of gold, illuminating manuscripts with gold ink, and dying hair a bright blonde. Thus it can be associated with artifice and fool's gold.

Physicians of Myddfai in Wales said, "If you would be at all times merry, eat saffron in meat or drink, and you will never be sad; but beware of eating over much, lest you die of excessive joy" (Watts 336). Saffron the woman indeed brings happiness and pleasure to her "many husbands," but too long an association can lead to their deaths.

Saffron was most popular as a spice in cooking, though the fishermen of Cornwall viewed it as unlucky, and feared that if they carried food with saffron, they would catch nothing. It was a necessary component in a great many dishes, from French bouillabaisse to Spanish paella, suggesting versatility and many forms. It was also known for being exotic and costly (Watts 335). Ironically, the plant is associated with the Buddhist paradise because of the saffron-robed holy monks (Shepherd 250). Evil spirits were frightened of saffron, particularly its bright color. Thus, Saffron the character bears a potential for good and holiness, much like Spike on *Buffy*, but will have a long road to achieve it.

In "Trash" (F1.11) Mal discovers her rich husband calls her Yolanda and his friend Monty calls her Bridget. (Yolanda is an elegant name and Bridget a more salt-of-the-earth name – she appears to adapt for each situation.) She assumes a different personality with each husband and never reveals the truth to her name or real motivations. "Rather than provide a key to her character – troubled childhood, mental illness, Iago-like spite – she cannot be pinned down to any one identity but instead cycles through numerous possible identities" (Beadling 58). By episode end, Mal is calling her "Yo-Saf-Bridge," making the point that all three names are equally ludicrous. Of course, unlike Darla and Lily, she chooses the names for herself rather than letting others name her. Her ethics appear lost and she might be directionless, but she's far less vulnerable than most of Whedon's nameless women.

Stitch Hessian
Hessian means something or someone is from an area of Germany – Hessian mercenaries fought for England during the American Revolution, and hessian bags are a rough burlap fabric. Both names are excellent for the mercenary and smuggler Jayne once betrayed ("Jaynestown," F1.7). Stitch matches with the fabric meaning, while sounding a bit parodic – in fact, he may be

a spoof on one-eyed Snake Plissken of the "Escape From" movie franchise.

Mr. Universe
Mr. Universe names himself this because his signals send and receive through the universe. He boasts, "There's the truth of the signal. Everything goes somewhere and I go everywhere." It's a hacker name and camouflage – the *Serenity* film novelization explains, "Like the operative, Mr. Universe had no real name that could be found" (218).

His love-bot wife Leonore is named for her most famous namesake – the dead wife from Poe's *The Raven*. Ironically, it's Mr. Universe that dies, with Leonore left to record his last words and carry on.

Firefly Family Members

Emma Washburne
In the *Serenity* comics, Zoe gives birth to a healthy girl after her husband's death, naming her Emma (after jokingly naming her Hoban after her father). The name Emma is Germanic for whole or universal. Thus life gives birth to the universe, and Emma brings completion to Zoe and the crew. While the name seems sweetly domestic, famous feminists have borne the name, especially Emma Peel, one of the earliest and most beloved TV action heroines.

Gabriel and Regan Tam
Gabriel and Regan Tam are River and Simon's parents. As shown in "Safe" (F1.5), they're conservative, wealthy people who don't understand their genius children and leave Simon to protect his sister unsupported.

The most famous literary Regan is from *King Lear* (source of the most famous literary Cordelia). This Regan offers the appearance of filial love and loyalty for her father, but fails when she's asked to support him, instead callously reduces his honor guard. Regan Tam appears to love her children, but when Simon begs them to risk their careers, wealth, and reputations to rescue River, they refuse.

Gabriel is named for the archangel of the Bible, who was not only a messenger but also a warrior for God. His name means *God is my strength*. In his short appearance on the show (in flashback), Gabriel Tam is the voice of conformity. Whedon's symbolism often shows Christian icons as more conformist and Pagan icons as part of the rebellious group of misfits seeking safety and love in his many shows. Thus Gabriel is a warrior for the establishment, who refuses to rebel and rescue River.

Radiant Cobb

Radiant Cobb is Jayne's mother. He seems devoted to her, as he sends her money (shown in "The Message," F1.12) and she sends him his famous knitted hat. In the comic *Better Days,* he names the ship of his dreams the *Radiant Cobb* for her. While she lives on a humble frontier planet, her name suggests her worth isn't tied to money but to motherly love and the warm home she creates. It's a sort of reverse Puritan name, extolling beauty rather than virtue, though it still retains a Puritan trace, like the frontierwoman Patience.

Planets in the *Firefly* 'Verse

The named planets of the 'Verse (taken from J. Chris Bourdier's "The Verse in Numbers") fall into identifiable categories, excepting those with more prosaic frontier-style names (Lux, Deadwood, Meridian, Shadow, Meadow, Newhope, Triumph):

- Norse myth: Himinbjorg, Aesir, Hastur, Freya, Beowulf, Alberich, Odin, Hammer, Brisingamen. Regions include Jormungand.
- Indian Myth: Sahadeva, Bhima, Yudhishtira, Nakula, Nirodha, Shiva, Rama, Ganesha, Yama, Vishnu. Regions include Raksasha and Qundalini's coils.
- Greek Myth: Aphrodite, Persephone, Belleraphon,

Selene, Poseidon, Hades, Ares, Calliope, Daedalus, Eris, Tethys, Priam, Vesta, Zephyr, Thalia, Hera, and the moon Zeus. Regions include Achilles, Agamemnon, Hippolyta's Belt.

- Aztec myth: the region Quetzacoatl
- Buddhist Precepts: Nirodha, Dukkha, Magga, Samudaya
- Bible and Christianity: St. Lucius, Iscariot, Lazarus, Ezra, Valentine, New Canaan, Moab, Ugarit. Regions include Mizpah.
- Classical Place Names: Ariopolis, Alexandria, Ithaca, Athens, Rubicon, Delphi
- China: Sihnon (Whedon calls this "a bastardization of Sino, our word for 'Chinese'"), Penglai (a city and mountain), Jiangyin (a city), Qin Shi Huang (an emperor), Shenzhou (a painter), Gonghe (a regency that ruled the Chinese Zhou Dynasty), and so on.
- British Ancient Place Names: Londinium, Albion, Avalon, St Albans, Aberdeen, Salisbury, Colchester, Kerry
- Shakespeare: Caliban, Ariel, Miranda, Oberon, Puck, Bottom, Lear
- Fannish Literature: Mycroft, Heinlein, Nautilus, Murphy
- Famous People: Muir, Disraeli, Whittier
- Just for Fun: Illyria, Angel, Fury

Dollhouse

In Los Angeles, the Rossum corporation rents out the bodies of its "actives," humans who have given up their bodies for five years. When not on assignment, they are mindless "dolls" identifiable only by NATO code names, though something of their original identities remain.

Dollhouse Main Characters

The Actives' names are borrowed from the NATO Phonetic Alphabet. (The other Dollhouse seen names its characters for the Greek Pantheon). The NATO alphabet denigrates the dolls into mere "things" – Whiskey is a drink that pleases men as they use it up, and Topher smilingly notes that "Kilo" weighs no more than her name, before using her in his experiments. Only Echo, named for a Greek nymph as well as a natural phenomenon, manages to end the oppression.

Each doll name conceals a "real" name and its personality beneath, along with an entire story of identity, struggle, and often exploitation. Too, there are the personas like Mellie or Doctor Saunders who become more real than the true one. This leaves viewers off-balance, hesitating whether to root for the loving Mellie or miserable Madeline to regain their shared body. But even the choice of nicknames reveals symbolism and depth of character, along with the series' constant dualism and reflection, foreshadowing their futures for the discerning.

Adelle DeWitt

While DeWitt means "white," it sounds in English as if the

head of the Dollhouse is "Adelle of wit," Adelle the witty. Indeed, she is clever and conniving as well as proper and formal. She is also a rebel against the hierarchy above her, and thus a mirror for one of the name's most famous holders:

> In the Netherlands of the 17th century the name was the most well known in the land. It came to be synonymous with power struggles between the civil authorities represented by Jan DeWitt (1625 – 1672) and his brother Cornelius, who each held the rank of Grand Pensionaries in the then republic of the states of Holland, and William 11nd, prince of Orange, the hereditary stadtholder or president. William was successful and the DeWitt brothers paid with their lives. (SurnameDB)

The meaning of white is interesting as Adelle begins the show as a "black hat," oppressing and using the dolls even as she claims to protect them. By "Epitaph 2" (D2.13), she's revealed herself to be a "white hat" in truth, content with a simple farming life beyond the reach of Rossum. The origins of the surname may lie in descriptions of blond-headed people, or quite possibly as a label for the marauding Vikings who raided and stole people's livelihoods, a parallel for Adelle as she steals their bodies. This Dutch name among so many British names of Whedon's emphasizes her outsider status – she is the overseer of Dolls and handlers, but not one of them.

Adelle means "noble," and is a French diminutive of Adelaide. It's a name as stately as its meaning, as the queen of the Dollhouse always appears regal – she is never known by diminutives such as Addie. St. Adelaide, who died in 999, was a princess involved in Otho the Great's struggle for the crown. Bartered as a marriage pawn in several alliances, St. Adelaide slipped from the Castle of Garda where she was confined and lived in freedom for some time. When Otho the Great invaded Italy, he wed Adelaide and achieved a stable rule by capitalizing on her popularity. The Rossum founders use Adelle DeWitt thus, to win over the ordinary citizens and solidify their rule.

Adelle finally escapes her keepers and finds a safe haven.

Adelaide was a careful ruler, who acted as regent and tried to bring peace and convert others to her cause. During the reign of her son Otho II, Adelaide's troubles in leadership began, mostly because of the jealousy of her daughter-in-law, Theophano, and also because of her excessive liberality in her works of charity. Adelle DeWitt is known for her charity projects, and she rules the Dollhouse well, all until Echo begins to subvert it from within.

Alpha/Carl William Kraft

Alpha, of course is an Alpha Male, handsome and strong, always in control. However, he is fragmented with far too many personalities, all of them laid shakily over a psychotic murderer. He will never be first in the alphabet of dolls, since Echo, whom he names "Omega," the ending, will always defeat him. And she is his creation, his deliberate mirror, his benevolent shadow. When Alpha downloads thirty-eight personalities into Echo to make her Eve to his Adam (note linguistic similarities between these pairs of names), he also alludes to Revelations: "I am the Alpha and the Omega, the First and the Last, the Beginning and the End" (22.13). As he bookends the Bible this way, he casts himself as God – Adam and Eve are taking forbidden knowledge, trying to become gods themselves. As Alpha tells Echo, "We're not just human anymore" ("Omega," D1.12). But Echo rejects his superiority and returns to the Dollhouse, welcomed back into paradise, even with her new knowledge intact. She is determined to bring knowledge to all her community, restoring their personalities and freedom. And she manages this, bringing about the Omegalike ending in the show's epitaph. Though Alpha is Echo's creator, he finally becomes her, turning from his murderous former self into a defender of the dolls in "Epitaph Two" (D2.13). At last, she has become destroyer (admittedly of Rossum) and he has become preserver.

In "Omega" (D1.12), Alpha's original name is revealed as Carl William Kraft. Ballard notes, "Three names, always ominous." Sociopathic "Terry Marion Karrens" from "Belle Chose" (D2.3) is the same. Of course, in American culture, murderers are generally publicized with all three names, to avoid confusion with other people sharing that name.

"Kraft" suggests craftiness, along with an identity as a builder and creator...in fact, the builder of the Dollhouse Stephen Kepler is Alpha is disguise. Carl is a variant on "Charles"...and interestingly, so is Caroline. Besides their Alpha and Omega connection, they share a subtle link, both transcending their programming to become much more. "Charles," from the French means "free man." Alpha is all-too free, free to murder, kidnap and torture with no one prepared to stop him.

William is another repeat name of Whedon's, seen in Spike's original name, along with variants Willow and Liam (Angel). It means "resolute protection" and emphasizes the syllable "will" for willpower. Alpha is free will incarnate, the freedom to pursue violence and listen to the destructive voices within. But by "Epitaph 2," he becomes the "resolute protector" in truth, leaving the Dollhouse so he can defend its inhabitants with his absence.

Boyd Langdon
Boyd is (oddly) Scottish for blond, while Langdon is a place name associated with Devonshire, Dorset, Essex, Kent and Warwickshire in England. The place name means "the long hill," derived from the Old English pre 7th Century "lang, long," long, with "dun," hill, down, mountain (SurnameDB). Langdon's rulership over a long hill evokes the patriarchy and the stretching towers of Rossum corporation, rather than the Dollhouse, a feminine place concealed underground.

Though it's unlikely Whedon intended this, the jarring name suggesting a blond British origin for a Black American suggests that Boyd Langdon is not what he seems – a traitor or spy with a hidden agenda. This of course turns out to be the truth. As Wilcox notes, "His persona has been no more real than a doll's imprint (though that statement is, of course, more complex than it might seem)" ("Echoes of Complicity").

Christopher "Topher" Brink

In many interviews and commentaries, Whedon is compared to the stories' architects, like geeky Topher the dolls' "programmer" or to the scientists of *Cabin in the Woods.* He notes, "Everyone thinks, 'Oh, Joss is Topher because he plays with the toys, he creates these personalities and then he wipes them away and he's amoral'" ("Vows" DVD Commentary). Whedon notes he has more in common with Adelle DeWitt, the director of the Dollhouse, because she is the "leader, [who] makes the hard choices" ("Vows" DVD Commentary).

Topher, like Xander, is the science fiction fan, the character most like the audience. Richard P. Steeves notes in "Dollhouse's Topher Brink: Man of Science, or Satan in a Sweater Vest?":

> Fans at a *Dollhouse* convention would likely prove to be intelligent, talkative, filled with nervous energy, at times socially awkward (especially among the opposite sex), show a predilection for energy drinks and sugary snacks, loving gaming, computers, movies and television, and even dress in a manner that is contrary to current fashion. In short, they are far more likely to have share a connection with Topher Brink than, say, a strong, confident FBI agent, a successful and powerful businesswoman, or a mind-wiped active.

Thus, as science fiction everyman, Topher is an echo of Joss Whedon and the fans. Like Whedon he designs the characters, gives them weaknesses as well as strengths, and even writes the characters' scripts. "It's not a shock to see a lot of Topher in myself, because he's building people, and he's amoral and fairly goofy," Whedon answers, as people make this comparison over and over (Goldberg).

Steeves adds: "The name Topher, surely, is a

diminutive form of Christopher, utilizing the second part of the given forename. Not nearly as common as 'Chris,' it deliberately echoes another Joss Whedon character who also uses the less-common, second half nickname." This, of course, is Alexander "Xander" Harris. Both characters are geeky and awkward, particularly around the opposite sex. And so both names suggest a childish social sigma, as they deliberately distance themselves from the social norm.

Christopher means "Christ-bearer"; thus, Topher simply means bearer. While he spends the first season happily oblivious to consequences for his science, the moral repercussions do in fact begin to weigh on him. In season two, he's more hesitant, asking Echo's permission to imprint her and feeling terrible remorse on discovering he has aided in Priya's rape and forcible condemnation to the Dollhouse. In "Epitaph 2" (D2.13), he indeed becomes the bearer of the cross, slowly building the device that will destroy him, carrying it to a high place, and setting it off, restoring the world through his sacrifice.

"But far more interesting than his first name is the surname of the character. What, then, is Topher on the Brink of? A scientific revolution? A mental breakdown?" (Steeves). Though he spends "Epitaph" on the brink of sanity, he is also on the cusp of manhood. In the first few episodes, he's constantly set against the moral Doctor Saunders, highlighting his own lack of morality. He is genius without fetters or fears for consequences. However, he begins to see the dolls as people, and this changes everything. Like Xander, he potentially has a great deal of growth ahead, or would have in a longer series.

Echo/Caroline Farrell

Echo is more than a letter in the NATO alphabet. In *Dollhouse*, it's her ability, to take on this personality or that one and "echo" it. "There is no me...I'm just a container. You think anybody would worship us? Be like worshiping a cup," she says in "Omega" (D1.12). She considers herself an empty vessel, "just the porch light" waiting for Caroline

However, as it turns out, being an Echo or empty vessel is her superpower. When Alpha downloads 38 personalities into her, she doesn't go mad, but absorbs them all. "That's her power – filling herself with souls until her sum is a far far greater whole" (Frankel, *Dollhouse 74*). She's soon ordering extra abilities from Topher and switching them on and off at will. She saves her friends from the Attic because, as she puts it, "I'm not normal. So I think I can do this."

Langdon tells her in "The Hollow Men," (D2.12), "You're going to be the savior of the world" because of this ability, existing in her spinal fluid.

> As the newly risen messiah of "Epitaph Two," Echo leads her people to Safe Haven. In fact, she enfolds her community in the shelter of herself – the Dollhouse that, like her, is a haven for lost souls. As she is a vessel, so is the Dollhouse, guarding all the personalities and uniting them into a great assemblage of power. (Frankel, *Dollhouse* 75)

With her echoing power, she fights for and redeems the world.

In the Greek myth, the nymph Echo loved the vain Narcissus. Unrequited, she faded away until all that was left was the sound of her voice. Paul Ballard does appear to love Echo. Still, he hesitates to be with her because he fears she's weak, just a voice or an "echo" of a personality.

Caroline ironically means "free man" (in a name related to Charles). "I wanna do everything. Is that so much to ask?" she says in the first episode, eager to embrace all aspects of life. Of course, she spends nearly the entire series trapped on a disk, unable to act. It's Echo who convinces her she needs to fight for her freedom:

> ECHO: Why do you have to go back in the wedge? Why don't you come home?
> CAROLINE: I *did* sign a contract.
> ECHO: I have thirty-eight brains. Not one of them thinks you can sign a contract to be a slave. Especially now that we have a black President.

> CAROLINE: [surprised] We have a black president? OK,
> I am missing everything. ("Omega," D1.12)

In fact, Caroline never regains her body, strictly speaking. Echo is in charge, and too strong for Caroline to rule her body, though she gains freedom from the Dollhouse in time. With her Irish last name, she may possibly be named for Kat Farrell, a reporter in the Marvel Comics' who tries to root out government conspiracies much like Caroline. She's suspicious of superheroes and tries to bring them down, in favor of the ordinary people who offer real heroism. Similarly, Echo advances her normal friends, like Tony and Priya, until Topher manages to remake the world.

Melly/Madeline Costley/November

Madeline Costley is November's true name. Madeline as a name comes from Mary Magdalene. Little is known about her, as she has more screen time as Mellie and November. She's a terribly sad character, in perpetual mourning after her young daughter's death. Her last name hints at the prostitution the Dollhouse engages in, as it "sells" her doll self to Paul Ballard and makes her desperate to please him. Her first name also suggests prostitution, along with a perpetual sorrow for the loss of a man she can never have, Paul Ballard.

Mellie is a more important character to the story as she works with Paul to break down the Dollhouse and falls in love with him. One of literature's most famous "Mellys" comes from *Gone with the Wind*. She loves Ashley Wilkes with all her heart, though he's fascinated by the alluring, independent Scarlett O'Hara. Melly by contrast, is simply the "sweet" one, content to keep the house while Ashley lusts for Scarlett. On her deathbed, she selflessly gives them permission to be together. Likewise, Mellie on *Dollhouse* is flung into competition with Caroline, a damsel in distress Paul Ballard wishes to rescue. "There's no room for a real girl when you can feel Caroline beckoning," Joel Mynor notes ("Man on the Street," D1.6).

This Mellie is also terribly self-sacrificing:

> MELLIE: [after making love] I'm not gonna freak out on you.
> PAUL: Uhhhh... good?
> MELLIE: When you tell me this is all a mistake and we should forget it ever happened, I'm gonna be very cool. You're going to be bothered by how cool I am.
> PAUL: What if I don't say that?
> MELLIE: I'll still be cool, but not as cool. ("Man on the Street," D1.6)

Though she wants Paul to be in love with her, she works with him to save Caroline out of compassion. Paul in turn treats her badly after discovering she's a doll placed in his life to please him and spy on him. When Mellie (in her Mellie persona) is suddenly shot and dies tragically, she leaves the way clear for Echo and Paul. "Mellie takes the choice to kill herself rather than be used to kill Paul Ballard. He is thus responsible for helping her gain a sense of identity and yet simultaneously involved in her death" (Wilcox, "Echoes of Complicity").

Paul Ballard

The Biblical Paul was a zealous persecutor of Christians, who attempted to destroy the entire belief system. Famously, he was converted on the road to Damascus and became one of its most fervent supporters. Paul Ballard spends much of the first season trying to bring down the Dollhouse, but soon becomes Echo's handler and works for the institution he despised. Eventually he becomes a true insider, as he's transformed into a doll. "In spite of his views on the unnaturalness of the system, he chooses to accept life on those flawed terms" (Wilcox, "Echoes of Complicity"). Mellie tells him "I'm a program," but he responds, "So am I. I decided – it doesn't matter anymore. We feel what we feel" ("The Hollow Men" D2.12). He ends the series inside Echo's mind – he has been let into more than the savior's inner circle –he's inside the savior.

Ballard may come from the Anglo-Saxon for bald, or

the Welsh Ap Alard, meaning the "son of the fox." The latter makes more sense for Paul, the wily and clever fellow, who, though an outsider like the Welsh, roots his way into the heart of the Dollhouse.

Rossum Corporation
The "Rossum Corporation" is named for Karel Capek's play *RUR: Rossum's Universal Robots.* "Rossum is just a name, actually. From a play. Although technically you're not robots, it seemed to fit," the head of Rossum explains ("Getting Closer," D2.11). Capek invented the word "robot" and told a story of men and women with souls and gradual self-awareness who are nonetheless forced to serve others.

> When Alquist explains that he needs to dissect these Robots to find the answers, he is shocked when the Robot (neatly named "Primus," meaning "first") refuses to take the Robot modeled after Helena to the dissecting room. Rather, Primus pleads to be allowed to take her place. The Robot Helena also offers herself in the place of Primus, leading Alquist to marvel that the Robots already have souls. Alquist tells them to leave, referring to the pair as Adam and Eve (108). The play ends with Alquist's impassioned cry that life will not end (Koontz, "Czech Mate")

Alpha and Echo seem like an Adam and Eve pair in "Omega" (D1.12). Other similarities appear as well, especially in the ethics of the situation. "There appears to be an uncanny similarity between Čapek's "stamping-mill" for broken Robots and Whedon's infamous "Attic" for broken Dolls." (Koontz, "Czech Mate"). All the dolls are forced to escape and fight for human acknowledgement.

Victor and Sierra
Victor and Sierra are appropriately gendered names, more humanizing than many others of the twenty-six NATO Alphabet possibilities. They are our least secret dolls, the ones who are honest with the audience from the start (or nearly so), who tear our hearts with their vulnerable

ingenuousness as they crave protection from their exploiters. In commentary, Whedon mentions casting Victor's actor because of "the innocence in those big ol' eyes." "You were supposed to help me," a tearful Priya tells Topher, who can only apologize weakly for letting her be used ("Belonging," D2.4). "Dr. Saunders? How can I be my best, please?" asks a mutilated Victor ("Omega," D1.12).

But that isn't all these two characters share. Both were brainwashed and abused: Victor by the military and Sierra by her rapist. Topher describes Victor as "Afghanistan war vet, severe PTSD ... which we cured" ("Stop-Loss," D2.9). "Belonging" shows Sierra's origin story. Filthy rich Nolan Kenard covets her and tries to buy her with gifts, and then with an art show in her honor, stuffed with dolls hired to talk him up. He seems oblivious to the concept that some people can't be bought, and he drugs the young free thinker Priya into schizophrenia to steal her life. When DeWitt discovers this, she calls him "a raping scumbag one tick shy of a murderer" ("Belonging"). Victor, with his PTSD, and Sierra with her schizophrenia, are supposed to be poster-children for the Dollhouse – not only paid but generously healed of their afflictions by Rossum's superior brain science. But both are victims here. And as Caroline reminds us, even a cleaned slate can't ever be erased completely.

In the safety of the Dollhouse, Victor and Sierra find comfort. Though deprived of memory, they begin "grouping," falling in love even absent of memory. Victor in his imprint as boyfriend Roger can't remember Sierra, only a "love that transcends my very being" ("Stop-Loss"). Likewise, a newly-awakened Priya remembers a love Topher assures her is "real" ("Belonging"). Whedon describes Victor and Sierra as "one of the things we came up with early on." Their reaction to each other is "absolutely simple and primal ... not based on anything about her character or his; it's just she does something chemically to him that nobody else does." ("Man on the Street" Commentary). In poignant moments, they paint each other's' faces, hold hands, or share strawberries, resembling Adam and Eve in their innocent fondness. (As such, they provide an interesting counterpoint to the willful Alpha and Echo). Calling them Romeo and Juliet (both in the Military Alphabet) would have been amusing but probably too blatant.

Priya's schizophrenia shows us how to view these characters: they are most damaged because they're split. Victor and Sierra can have love or their memories, but to gain one is to forget the other. Even when they regain their true personalities, they have forgotten all the sweet moments of the Dollhouse and must relearn each other. This the Dollhouse has taken from them, and it can never be returned. Regaining memories means facing the shadow – the dark side of the self each sold away in return for peace and, as they had hoped, happiness. When Victor and Sierra regain their true personalities, they are consigned to the Attic, appropriate symbolically as they must face their deepest nightmares, even die, in order to escape. Once they manage this, they become warriors in Echo's cause, in full control of their memories and selves.

Priya, an Indian name, means "beloved." Her role on the show, of course, is to be Tony's soulmate. This exotic name for the exotic character (an Asian from Australia) emphasizes her marginalized status, leaving her open to exploitation. "Sierra," an Irish name meaning "dark" likewise suggests her exotic looks and hidden secrets. Her last name, Tsetsang, was invented by the actress.

Victor's real name is Anthony Ceccoli. Anthony means "praiseworthy," and links the character with Mark Antony, best known for his star-crossed romance with Cleopatra. He was also a rebel against Octavian Caesar in order to carve out in independent life for himself. His last name derives from "Franciscus," which came from "Frank," free man. This of course is Tony's goal as he leads a revolution in order to win freedom from the Dollhouse. Victor itself means conqueror, a strong matchup for the rest of his name.

Whiskey/Claire Saunders/Clyde 2.0

One of the most famous Claires was the medieval Saint Clare of Assisi. At age eighteen, she heard Saint Francis of Assisi speak and she left her privileged life as a noblewoman to live in humble poverty "after the manner of the holy Gospel." She cut her hair, donned a rough dress, and began a life of serving others. Claire Saunders and her transformation from free woman (whoever she was before) to doll mirrors this. St. Claire hid away in a cloister "hidden with Christ in God," where she practiced humility, poverty, and mortification (Robinson). After Saint Francis's death, Claire continued to follow his teachings slavishly. Whiskey on the show joins the Dollhouse and cloisters herself in her office, functioning as a guide for others even after Topher and the others have gone. St. Claire founded the Poor Clares, and her legacy lived on far after her death.

Saunders is probably derived from "Alexander," the great conqueror, with a name that means "Defender of Men." Doctor Saunders fights to defend and aid the dolls, but her quest is subverted when she's revealed to be one of them.

Claire means clearness, clarity. Sadly, to find such clarity, Claire must accept that this label is a lie – under Claire is Whiskey, and under whiskey is another woman, whose name is never revealed. Claire can also refer to the clarity of guidance. Whiskey (as Whiskey) does become a guide of this sort, in "Epitaph 1" (D1.13).

By contrast, Whiskey has a truly dehumanized name as alcohol deprives people of humanity and is specifically a thing designed for consumption. The Dollhouse has used and exploited Doctor Saunders: She (and the audience) remain unaware she's an artificial personality imprinted on the doll Whiskey until "Briar Rose" (D1.11) and "Omega" (D1.12) – when Dominic calls for "Whiskey," she naively assumes he wants a drink. (In that atmosphere, anyone ought to jump when hearing one of those twenty-six words). Once she was the most requested doll, but now the Dollhouse refuses to fix her scars, since it simply "isn't

137

necessary" (a particular slap compared with how Victor is coddled and healed from similar injuries). We see how damaged she is when she speaks to him, clearly referencing herself: "You're ugly now. You're disgusting. All you can hope for now is pity" ("Omega").

Whedon describes Saunders in terms of the "Phantom of the Opera-like space in which she would lurk ... Actually she's twisted" ("Designing the Perfect Dollhouse"). Of course, the instincts that keep her hidden in her office, snipping at Topher, are programmed. But the trauma that slashed her is real, leaving her an abused woman fleeing from life, unwilling to face herself. She refuses to look at her file, insisting that she knows who she "really" is. In fact, as the two seasons stand, we never find out.

She is used once again at series end, imprinted as the evil Clyde 2.0, who has been programmed to follow orders, much as she has. As an active, she was the "best," but all her following incarnations reflect the scars on her face: she is flawed, damaged, a body to be used when necessary. In "The Hollow Men" (D2.12), Echo defeats her and she is carried from Rossum, her real identity still unseen. She is the perpetual reflection of Rossum's worst, with nothing behind it.

Poor Whiskey drifts through the series, used by Topher, by Langton, even by Echo (as she guides people to Safe Haven but leaves Whiskey behind to go mad). She finally dies as Whiskey, defending the Dollhouse that took everything from her, never reintegrated.

Dollhouse Guest Characters

Bennett Halverson

Bennett is an English and Irish surname related to Benedict, "blessed." This seems ironic as she's lost the use of her arm after her friend betrayed her. However, she has more power than she knows, as one of the programmers of the Dollhouse. She need only acknowledge that she has blessings, rather than throwing them away.

Halverson, from Norse-Viking and Scandinavian origins, is a patronymic, from "son of Halvor," meaning prudent. Halverson is indeed practical about her interests, while the non-British name marks her as a bit of an outsider. This uncompromising woman has two men's names, marking her as hard and emotionally unavailable. She is cast as a Final Girl, with androgynous name and mostly asexual lifestyle (in contrast with popular Echo/Caroline), though in an inversion of the classic tropes, she dies while the sexual Caroline returns to consciousness and saves the world.

Clyde Randolph/Clyde 2.0/Arcane

Clyde is one of Rossum's co-founders. Clyde, a Scottish place name, is also a Welsh name meaning "hardy" and "fair." The most famous person of this name was the thief of Bonnie and Clyde. Clyde Randolph is indeed a (body) thief, and quite "hardy" as he exists in multiple bodies, basically immortal.

Randolf is from the Germanic personal name made of rand (shield rim) and "wolf." As such, Clyde is a warrior, a wolf among the sheep, as well as an outsider with a Germanic name. His successor, Clyde 2.0, is a creepy pun on the new software and "upgrades" of today's world.

In the horrific Attic, Clyde 2.0 is known as Arcane, with the visage of a monster. "Arcane" means secret or hard to comprehend, and in fact, Clyde has the arcane knowledge of what the Attic truly is and how to bring down Rossum.

Daniel and Cindy Perrin

Daniel means "God is my judge," a firm upstanding name that's Oz's first name and Willow's middle name, also used by avenging "angel" Daniel Holtz. (This repeat name may slyly point to the fact that he's played by Alexis Denisof from *Buffy* and *Angel*). Daniel Perrin turns into a similar avenging angel when he becomes aware of how the Dollhouse has used him, or at least he tries. According to

"Epitaph," he becomes president, using his drive and crusading strength to push himself to the top.

Perrin is a French/British surname that's a variant on Peter, rock. Cindy and Daniel act as the "rock" and perfect "pairing" for each other until the truth is discovered, that they are doll and handler.

Cindy, meanwhile, is usually short for Cynthia, or occasionally even Cinderella. The latter possibility nods to Daniel and Cindy's script:

> CINDY: Remind me why I love you so much.
> DANIEL: I'm your white knight.
> CINDY: And I'm your beautiful damsel.
> DANIEL: Ever after. ("The Public Eye," D2.5)

Cindy is a popular American name, harmless and girly. It appears in *The Brady Bunch, Jimmy Neutron,* and even Doctor Seuss. In Britain, Sindy is a doll, competitor to the American Barbie. (Though the name also contains the syllable "sin" as seen in the Marvel supervillainess Synthia Schmidt, aka Sin). Like many Whedon characters including Melinda Mae, April, and Iris, her girlish name conceals great strength and power, along with secrets and violence.

Laurence Dominic

His last name sounds like "dominion," part of the establishment like Adelle. Laurence is a Roman name "from the place of Laurels." Laurence is indeed defender of his home "place," the Dollhouse. Ironically, when he is given a reward (the original use of laurel leaves as a celebratory crown among Greeks and Romans), it's a trip to the Attic.

Iris

Iris is a Whedon staple – the innocent-looking little girl who's actually an evil murderer. While her name comes from the pretty, delicate flower, it also suggests part of the eye, emphasizing a need to look beyond the surface. Like Topher's assistant Ivy, Iris has a name that sounds like a

NATO alphabet name, another clue to the audience that she's been imprinted. Iris was the name of the Greek rainbow goddess, a beautiful figure who carried souls to the other world, much as little Iris does. The iris flower ironically symbolizes faith and friendship, while the blade shape suggests a hidden strength and ferocity. Iris is in fact a blade hidden inside a sweet flower of a girl, one that will kill all her allies.

Ivy
The ivy, because it is evergreen, has always been identified with fidelity and immortality. It clings to its support, a symbol of attachment and undying affection. Ivy is, of course, Topher's endlessly loyal assistant. Though her name isn't part of the NATO alphabet, it sounds as though it could be, linking her with the obedient dolls who are toys at the whim of Topher the supergenius. If the show had continued, she might have been revealed as a doll or made into one. Topher finally begs her to leave him, adding "don't become me." As she does, his ideas live on in her, and he gains a type of immortality through his protégé.

Mag
Mag, played by Felicia Day, is a character from the future apocalypse. Her name, though short for Margaret, matches the tough nicknames of her team like Zone and Griff. Margaret means pearl, emphasizing the hidden value of innocent, girlish looking Mag, who becomes a warrior nonetheless.

Zone
Zone's name, a battle or apocalypse nickname, ironically sounds like the Dolls' NATO names. While he seeks a future free from "tech," he's being manipulated, and is more like the dolls than he realizes. His name, suggesting a militarized space, emphasizes his quest for Safe Haven – a safe zone in the battle.

Agents of S.H.I.E.L.D.

This is the Avengers' support staff: Agent Phil Coulson, back from the dead, leading a team of two fighters, two scientists, and an expert hacker. As they battle to save the world's innocents from supervillains and rogue tech, they prove they can be just as tough as the big guys. Whedon didn't contribute any characters to *The Avengers:* even Maria Hill is from the comics, like all the others. Coulson was invented for the *Iron Man* movie. Still, *Agents of S.H.I.E.L.D.* has allowed him to fill the world with many original characters along with comic book staples.

Agents of S.H.I.E.L.D. Main Characters

Grant Douglas Ward

This manly man has a monosyllabic name. Grant is a generic masculine name meaning "tall" – which he certainly is. One of the most famous Grants, the U.S. president, was general during the Civil War, and Grant Ward is caught in a similar battle. Oddly, he is not anyone's "ward" (except John Garrett's) but Skye and the entire team are considered his.

The other meaning of ward, setting a watch, is likely more accurate. He's presented as a company man, believing unquestioningly in S.H.I.E.L.D. and its hierarchy of command, in contrast with skeptical Skye and increasingly disillusioned Coulson. As season one finally reveals, his true watch has been on behalf of H.Y.D.R.A. as he's spied on his team and awaited H.Y.D.R.A.'s rise. He describes his old personality to Garrett as false – a "cover" unlike his true self, while fans agree that his true personality surpasses the featureless old one.

"Douglas" means dark water, from the Scottish, emphasizing the deep well of his childhood bullying and the beneath-the-surface darkness within him.

On *Buffy*, Riley says he basically grew up in a Grant Wood painting – woods, a dog, cabin, Iowa ("Pangs," B4.8). It's generic, classic, trustworthy America. Grant's name, a few letter off from this, indicates a similar childhood and similar reliability. He shows no particular interest in art, and thus he's linked with Riley, another soldier for a secure government organization. Riley in fact turns traitor to his beloved unit and the entire Initiative, for the sake of someone he loves.

Jemma Simmons

Jemma is an Italian name, very popular in 1980s England, around the time of the character's birth. From a medieval Italian nickname for a precious gem, Jemma was the name of Dante's wife and was borne by a nineteenth century saint.

Precious stones are not only an image of wealth – their marvelous colors stimulate the imagination. These crystals were often used for mediation or focusing of magic (as Giles does with Buffy in "Helpless," B3.12); thus polished gems can serve as mirrors. Mirrors in ancient times symbolized the soul, and could be used, people thought, for seer powers and astral projection. Venus is seen gazing into her mirror, not through vanity, but through the power it represents.

"Throughout the world, these stones in general, since they reveal their beauty only when they are cut and polished, came to symbolize humanity itself in its need for refinement" (Biedermann 272). Gems are the beauty and mystery of the natural world that must be polished and shaped by mankind – an excellent representation for the natural sciences Jemma studies through the lens of her extensive training. Her name also nods to Gemini, the twins, as she's "half" of Fitz.

Simmons comes from the ancient Hebrew Shimon, to hearken. As a surname, it hails from England, where the family held an ancient seat in Cornwall and Devon. Their crest is yellow and black quarters, with three-leaved clovers (SurnameDB). So far, Jemma seems lucky as she's remained safer than most of her team members. As a big sister and listener to most of the crew (not just Fitz) she does indeed harken to others as well as to the sciences.

Leopold "Leo" Fitz

The meaning of the name Leopold is "Bold people" or possibly lion. Leo in the first season doesn't appear to live up to his name, just as Xander is not yet a great leader. Thus the shorter nicknames rather than the signifiers of kings and conquerors, Alexander and Leopold, indicate immaturity but also room to grow. Both must evolve into these roles as the series progresses.

The Zodiac symbol Leo is the lion. It is known for creative force, a suitable match for the tech genius and weapons expert. It also suggests a love of action and strong nature. The lion is generally a masculine symbol, associated with the sun. In heraldry, it's the "king of beasts" suggesting strength and valor (Biedermann 210). Likewise, Fitz is a blend of strength and creativity – intellect rather than battle skills, yet with a clever ingenuity that saves the day on multiple occasions.

When Ward and Fitz go on a mission together in "The Hub" (AS1.7), Ward is surprised that Fitz successfully gets them out of messes, refuses to save himself at his "bodyguard's" expense, and insists that he was told to look after Ward, not merely to be his burden. The seeds of the lion are clearly there.

The surname Fitz meant the illegitimate son – "Fitz-william, Fitz-gerald," etc. This name, aside from revealing his British origin, may emphasize his troubled upbringing. Fitz's home life hasn't been shown yet, but it's likely he fits perfectly among the misunderstood young people whose parents find them a mystery: Willow, Xander, Wesley.

Fitz-Simmons

Fitz-Simmons are most often discussed as a joint entity – they are the science team and example of a perfect partnership before they are individuals. Producer Maurissa Tancharoen comments, "Fitz-Simmons was one of the first ideas we had, of having a character you think is one person but then when you meet them you realize it's two people [Iain De Caestecker·and Elizabeth Henstridge]" (Bahr). In fact, in much of classic television, this was the pompous butler's name, hyphenated like Wesley Wyndam-Pryce.

Jed Whedon adds, "Fitz-Simmons are so used to only working with each other, they don't have the social skills to ingratiate themselves to a stranger" (Bahr). They are insular and understand each other instantly – the perfect team. In zodiac signs, Gemini or the twins represent a perfect balance. Fitz-Simmons appear to be a symbolic brother-sister pair like Willow and Xander or Mal and Zoe.

Twins represent "the twofold nature of all beings and the dualism of their physical and spiritual, diurnal and nocturnal tendencies" (Chevalier and Gheerbrant 1047). As such, they symbolize man's innate contradictions. Fitz and Simmons are not opposites in their shared cheerful naive personalities, but in their professions: Simmons is female and works with life sciences (human and alien), while Fitz is male and works with engineering and weapons. They are Hephaestus and Demeter, the inventor and the nurturer. As a united team, they often disagree about methods, with their opposite training coming into conflict. As they choose, they represent one part of the soul or motivation taking priority over another.

Each zodiac symbol has a gem associated: the gem for Gemini is a diamond, thus combining Leo and Jemma may equal a diamond ring, symbolically (Biedermann 273).

Melinda Qiaolian "The Cavalry" May

Melinda May's name smacks of countrified girlishness – it sounds like something that might be found in *Tom Sawyer* or *Anne of Green Gables* if it were a set of first and middle names. Even as first and last name, the association lingers. Melinda as a name hails from eighteenth century poetry, along with Belinda, Clarinda, Dorinda and Florinda. It was popular in the U.S. in the late 1960s and 1970s, belonging to notable people from philanthropist Melinda Gates to Melinda in *Ghost Whisperer*.

Of course, Melinda May subverts this naming pattern completely: she is in fact not Middle American or eighteenth century British, but Asian-American. Further, she is hardly the "girl next door" but instead a powerhouse of taciturn fighting skill. Her harmless-sounding name in contrast with her physical strength harkens notably back to Buffy. Further, her names are alliterative like many characters in superhero fiction (Lois Lane, Lex Luthor, Peter Parker). She is the superhero of the plane, not just its pilot.

She's nicknamed "The Cavalry" after she destroyed an enemy force all by herself and rescued her trapped fellow agents. The meaning is clear – one can call for the cavalry, and if she shows up, that's enough. She hates the nickname, possibly because it's dehumanizing or possibly because of what the adventure cost her.

> COULSON: She took it upon herself to get them out. Said she could fix the problem. So she went in, crossed off the enemy force. Didn't say how.
> SKYE: Did she lose anyone in there?
> COULSON: Herself. ("Repairs" AS1.9)

In "The Only Light in the Darkness," (AS1.19), she mentions her middle name is Qiaolian. With a meaning of "always skillful," it matches well with Melinda's abilities – she is indeed a one woman army. In *Iron Man: Titanium #1*, a villainous representative from Advanced Idea Mechanics (the research division of H.Y.D.R.A. that appears in *Iron Man 3*) named Huang Qiaolian is introduced. Some fans wonder if her mother, from the same episode, is a member.

Phil Coulson
Coulson was not invented by Whedon's team, but as the

leader, he has an important place in the series. Phil literally means "love" (probably from Philip, lover of horses, but he's notably never called that). His last name is an Anglicization of the Gaelic "MacCumhaill," son of Cumhall, meaning champion, or possibly from a pet form of Nicholas, which means "victory of the people." Thus he is champion of the people, protector of those who can't protect themselves, as he insists in "The Only Light in the Darkness," (AS1.19). He's also the surrogate father and the team's heart.

Skye

Skye chose to name herself (a sign of independence, especially in Whedon's works) after the orphanage named her "Mary Sue Poots" ("The Only Light in the Darkness," AS1.19). While this is a subtle, fannish joke, Skye is very much a "Mary Sue," a term for fanfiction where the author creates a "perfect" stand-in for themselves. As TV Tropes defines it:

> The prototypical Mary Sue is an original female character in a fanfic who obviously serves as an idealized version of the author mainly for the purpose of Wish Fulfillment. She's exotically beautiful, often having an unusual hair or eye color, and has a similarly cool and exotic name. She's exceptionally talented in an implausibly wide variety of areas, and may possess skills that are rare or nonexistent in the canon setting. She also lacks any realistic, or at least story-relevant, character flaws – either that or her "flaws" are obviously meant to be endearing.

This "always right" girl who out-hacks the government, outwits Ward, and dodges bad guys seems to fit well, even before her mystery origin is revealed. It seems protecting her was S.H.I.E.L.D.'s high priority when she was young – in a real way, she's the center of the universe.

Meanwhile, Skye, with no last name, is an enigma, to herself as well as to her team. Her single name, as a real English word, might function as a code name or hacker name, like Neo and Trinity in *The Matrix.* It's revealed early that she joined in order to discover her origins. Midway through season one, they are revealed – she is in fact an "084" and literally fell out of the sky! Her name has shared her truth with watchers from the beginning.

The sky generally symbolizes freedom and open space. Skye is an anti-conformist hacker before she abandons this role to join the team. It remains to be seen whether she will continue being a force of freedom or give in to the cage S.H.I.E.L.D. has already placed her in with her human identity and restrictive cuff. At the same time, it must be noted that, just as River dwells on a ship, Skye dwells on a plane. Both can thus be considered the avatar of their respective homes. When Skye codes the hard drive of the first season to only unlock at a certain height, she sets the plane as her home base rather than the café of her past life.

Heaven is often the top of hierarchical religious structure, with the Sky God (like Odin and his son Thor) ruling over all. "Heaven is the universal symbol of superhuman power, which may be either well-intentioned or to be feared" (Chevalier and Gheerbrant 485). Thus Skye, in Buffy-like style, may turn out to be more powerful than the hierarchies of Norse pantheon and S.H.I.E.L.D. alike. This "single concept brings together meteorology, astronomy, astrology, theology, and notions of the origin of the cosmos" (Biedermann 167). Skye is thus all this embodied. While she began as a hacker, she learns self-defense from Ward, and other skills will continue to develop.

Whether divided into the dichotomy of earth/sky or the four elements of alchemy and European medievalism, sky and air are masculine attributes. Whedon is no stranger to gender-flipping names and characteristics, especially with gentle Fitz and aggressive Melinda May. Skye may display more masculine attributes later on. Sky also often joins with earth in a mystical marriage. An "Earth" character is not evident, but may appear in a superhero with powers born from the ground below.

Agents of S.H.I.E.L.D. Guest Characters

Antoine "Trip" Triplett

Trip has a pair of French names, suggesting his background. Anthony and related names mean "praiseworthy," suggesting he's a good person. Jemma herself certainly praises him a lot, and vouches for him to get him on their team. His last name suggests he may become the "triplet" of the Fitz-Simmons pair – he's certainly interested in Jemma. His name suggests to some that Triplett will be the superhero Triathalon, an Olympic sprinter from the comics who seeks direction in the Triune Understanding, a philosophical movement that preaches balance of environment and self. For another possibility, the Hypno-Beam Trip produces in "Ragtag" (AS2.21) may be a nod to the Hypno-Hustler, an African-American Spider-Man villain named Antoine.

Trip is a logical nickname for the character's last name and for many third children through history. Famous fictional Trips include the perfect "nice guy" of *Enterprise* Commander Charles "Trip" Tucker III and heartthrob Trip Fontaine of *The Virgin Suicides,* These logically parallel for this hero, who's first introduced through Jemma's interest in him.

Audrey Nathan

This character is "the cellist," mentioned several times as Coulson's love before she appears in "The Only Light in the Darkness" (AS1.19), played by Amy Acker. Audrey means "noble strength," and she indeed acts as bait and lets Coulson go with a particular dignity. Her last name Nathan is a male first name meaning "he gave" in Hebrew – Nathan is a Biblical prophet. While she gives Coulson up, more may be coming from this character.

Clairvoyant/John Garrett

This mysterious enemy, known only by this label, is finally revealed to be the agent who's fought beside them,

Coulson's friend and Grant's mentor. He's also not in fact clairvoyant, only well briefed with intelligence. His mystery is much of what gave him power and allowed him to operate successfully for years. His Teutonic surname means "defender," though its German origin might give careful viewers a clue exactly which side he's defending. John, the most common male first name, suggests he's hiding his identity behind a nondescript life.

The Girl in the Flowered Dress/Raina

This nickname is the young woman's first identity, in the episode of that name. As such, she's a perfect mystery woman. Her association with flowers, beauty and the traditional feminine values marks her as an "assistant" rather than superpower in her own right. Eventually, her name is revealed as Raina, meaning queen...suggesting she's incomplete without her boss and king. This of course is the Clairvoyant in season one, though she appears to have other loyalties. In "Providence" (AS1.18), Garrett calls Raina "Flowers" repeatedly and sends her a silk dress with flowers, even as she protests that she has another identity. Flowers are feminine, soft, sweet, and harmless – he may be not-so-subtly trying to pigeonhole her into that role.

Ian Quinn

In Hebrew the meaning of the name Ian is Gift from God, while Quinn means "council." His attitude suggests both these qualities as he creates an empire of power and tries to recruit Skye to join him.

Mike Peterson/Deathlok

Mike Peterson has a friendly, folksy boy-next-door name before he reveals his superpowers. His transformation is shown step by step as his homey loving father side conflicts with the growing influence of Centipede. He receives one piece of "Deathlok" tech, then another, until he finally becomes known by the name of the tech, as he follows its agenda at every moment.

Miles Lydon

Skye's hacker boyfriend Miles has a name that means "merciful" or "soldier." He's fighting on the opposite side from S.H.I.E.L.D., though he does have compassion...Skye upon seeing him must choose a side in a test that strains her to the limit. Miles is in fact a liar and sell-out, as emphasized through his last name. While the name isn't strictly alliterative, the repeat vowels make it sound superhero-like. He may reappear as the show returns for a second season.

Comics

Fray

Fray is Whedon's first comic, starring a street thief centuries in the future – the first slayer born since Buffy's time. She receives the call of the chosen one while struggling to save her brother and face down her sister the cop, all in a dystopian Manhattan.

Melaka Fray

Far in a dystopian future, a new slayer is born. She is Fray, a street thief, with a personality that resembles Faith's. "She is hard, defensive, vulnerable, goofy, and yes, wicked sexy," Whedon notes ("Forward," *Fray*).

Melaka is a place name, conjuring images of earth that was and exotic desert locations, even as Melaka leaps through the ruins of Manhattan. Malacca Town, named for the Melaka or Malacca River, was founded in Malaysia two thousand years ago, lending its name to the modern country.

The name "Malacca" itself was derived from the fruit-bearing Malacca tree. According to the *Malay Annals*, legend has it that the king saw a mouse deer outrun his hunting dog when he was resting under the Malacca tree. He thought this boded well, remarking, "This place is excellent, even the mouse deer is formidable; it is best that we establish a kingdom here." Today, the mouse deer is part of modern Malacca's coat of arms. As a slayer, Melaka Fray dodges the powerful vampires through wit and skill, much like that tiny mouse deer. Though not as powerful as Buffy, she is a survivor.

The Arab merchants called the kingdom "Malakat" (Arabic for "congregation of merchants") because it was home to many trading communities. Malacca was a bustling international trading port, much like Melaka's Haddyn. Certainly, Melaka Fray is seen bartering, bargaining, and, yes, stealing as she struggles through urban life.

She goes by the more masculine "Mel" or "Fray" rather than the feminine Melaka, establishing herself as a rather androgynous character. This also provides parallels between her and Captain Mal. In Fray's world, names are shortened, as is the rest of language. Her first lines are a characteristically terse, "Bad day. Started bad. Stayed that way."

"Fray," like Kaylee's related "Frye," means "Free man." Melaka is certainly free – of social responsibility, laws, and family ties after her sister leaves for the world above and her brother is made a vampire. However, as they both return to plague her, she must remember she will never truly be free – she still has her family. She becomes a slayer and finally becomes a savior of her community, becoming part of it at last. "Fray" with Whedon's spelling also associates her with battles and conflict, as she battles the vampires for the defense of her people.

Erin Fray

Erin Fray is Melaka's older sister. With a long, blonde ponytail and job with the law enforcers of Haddyn, she's a voice of authority and proper behavior, just as Buffy is for Faith. Erin is a name for Ireland, also meaning peace, as Erin Fray struggles to calm Melaka's headstrong thieving as well as their family discord. It also resembles the Erinyes, the Greek Furies or Goddesses of Vengeance. "You took him on a grab [thieving job] and you got our brother killed," Erin lectures her scruffier sister. She continues to act as the voice of blame for Melaka as well as the voice of her conscience.

Harth Fray

"Like Buffy, Fray discovers the one she loves most has become a soulless vampire determined to destroy the world. This is not her lover, Angel, but her twin brother Harth, who inherited Fray's prophetic dreams. The pair is split, as Harth has the mental skills and Fray the physical" (Frankel, *Buffy* 195).

Harth is an Anglo-Saxon family name, for those who lived on the heath, or poor uncultivated soil. Their motto translates as "Hope for Better." As such, Harth's name reveals his humble origins in the dregs of the dystopian Haddyn, before he becomes a vampire. "I will open the gateway and bring the old ones back. And everyone you love will die screaming," he tells Mel (*Fray*). Thus he brings additional meaning to their last name Fray, conflict.

Icarus

The vampire Icarus is the one to transform Harth. He eventually begins serving Harth, whom he believes is the Chosen One of the vampires. In myth, Icarus was Daedalus's son. With homemade wings, he flew too near the sun and was burned to death. The name is synonymous with too much ambition, leading to destruction.

Runaways

This Marvel series stars a group of teens on the run from their evil parents. Led by Nico Minoru, they tangle with the classic heroes and villains of their world. In his *Dead End Kids*, Whedon has them leave L.A. for New York, then accidentally catapult back to 1907, to tangle with the superheroes, villains, and runaway teens of the distant past.

Klara Prast

Klara Prast (later known as Tower of Flower or Rose Red) is invented by Whedon. She's an abused twelve-year-old from the turn of the century, whom the Runaways bring back to modern times. Klara can "talk to" (as she puts it), plants. In fact, her name is a play on the word chloroplast, the plant cells that control photosynthesis. Klara Prast also parallels girl-power star Kitty Pryde.

Klara means bright or clear, while her last name (from her abusive husband) is from the German pravest, meaning "provost." With a word that means a university academic administrator and has also been used to mean an ostentatious person, her husband sets himself as the establishment.

Lillie McGurty/Spieler

In the classical world, as well as Christianity and alchemy, the lily symbolized chastity and purity, but also death, as it often appears at funerals (Shepherd 261). Unfortunately for Lillie in 1907, this proves all too accurate, as she's the romantic lead but fails to run away with Victor, a Runaway and her true love. She lingers into the future, elderly and consumed by loss.

"Like a lily among thorns is my darling among the young women," the *Song of Solomon* writes (2.2) In the Biblical tradition, the lily is the symbol of election of the beloved's choice (Chevalier and Gheerbrant 609). Unfortunately for Lillie, she fails to choose correctly. Fascinatingly, it's symbolically equivalent to the lotus which springs up from muddy waters as "a symbol of the potential of the individual to realize the antitheses of his or her being" (609). This is exactly Lillie's plot in *Runaways.*

Some ancient writers considered their suggestive shape and enticing scent more symbolic of romance than of purity: Persephone was gathering lilies when Hades dragged her down to hell, so they can symbolize a melding of temptation and the underworld. "A lily was what Apollo's catamite, Hyacynthius, was changed into and in this context, the flower evokes unlawful passion" (Chevalier and Gheerbrant 608). Lillie and Victor are star-crossed, and while they fall in love, they can never be together.

Her Irish surname is typical for turn-of-the-century

156

New York, especially for the lower class. It means strong and hard, but she fails to live up to all it suggests. While a "spieler" is literally an announcer or salesperson who talks up his product, the particular sound of the superhero name fits her as she spins, spirals, and unwinds in the air. It has an old-fashioned, haphazard quality to it, but in the end, she sells Victor a load of empty promises.

The Wonders

Whedon introduces a host of new characters from three rival gangs in 1907 New York.

The morally ambiguous Upward Path offers the witch Black Maria, who dresses in a nun's uniform and blends her Christian and pagan qualities down to her name. The Difference Engine is a staple of Steampunk, fitting perfectly into the setting and nodding to the historical invention and William Gibson novel of that name. Finally, the Witchbreaker as she calls herself is the great-grandmother of magical heroine Nico Minoru, who plans to test her until she succeeds or breaks.

The vicious Sinners have the cannibalistic Maneater (whom Nico disarms on multiple levels by transforming him into a vegan). Morphine, who hurls poison-filled syringes, and Forget-Me-Not, a mad girl staple of Whedon's – delicate, sensual, and unforgettably armed with an enticing scent.

The Street Arabs include many characters like the Runaways themselves: Lillie and Tristan, the flying boy who loves her (in Arthurian legend, Tristan is half of an epically doomed romantic pair, much like Romeo). Dead George Pelham, whose names of a farmer and a land in England mark him as a protector of their hideout, though he's also a zombie. Hoyden, a tomboy girl who takes pride in her unconventional status. Professor Duck, a Chinese scientist whose goofy personality echoes Mole and Gune from *Atlantis: The Lost Empire* and *Titan A.E.* (Whedon did script treatments on both). Finally, there's "the Swell," as he calls himself, until his magical stick is destroyed, metaphorically deflating him. His real name is Eddie Gunman, and he is indeed for hire.

Sugarshock

In this series, Dandelion and her friends defend an alien princess with a battle of the rock bands. It's light, silly, and short as a Whedon one-off.

Dandelion Naizen

Dandelion is the leader of her pals as well as her band. Dandelions are flowers like miniature suns, bursts of spiky yellow. As such, Dandelion is a figure of daylight and sunshine, much like Buffy and Dawn Summers. Nonetheless, Dandelion is not seen fighting vampires, in fact, she says she works for a secret government division, much like the Initiative.

The dandelion blooms year-round and is a plant sacred to Saint Brigit, patron of springtime. It's called the "little flame of God" in Gaelic (Watts 99). Dandelion clocks, as they're called when the seeds are blown, are a tool of prophecy, another link with the slayer.

The flower is a tough survivalist – it springs up in people's well-groomed orderly lawns no matter how they try to suppress it and hurls its plumed seeds through the world. The fiercely jagged tooth shapes bordering its leaves give it its original French name of *"Dent de Lion,"* (lion's tooth) later corrupted to "dandelion." Thus Whedon's heroine is another lioness, armed with toughness.

Naizen is an unusual Japanese first name for a boy. Written with kanji, it breaks down into "house/inside" and "table." Dandelion is guardian of the home as well as their band. Monks would often take on new names that were two-kanji compounds, with the kanji being read in the "Chinese" way rather than the "Japanese" way. Thus it appears to be made up from pieces, perhaps a nickname or assumed name, sounding something like Shepherd Book.

L'Lihdra

In their band, the tall L'Lihdra in pink pinstripes plays guitar, and plump Wade in a low-cut dress plays drums. The former name is alien and exotic, the latter is short and blunt, masculine coded rather than feminine. Wade emphasizes this role when she picks up a male groupie, noting, "You remember you're not allowed to talk until after I've used you for sex, right?" When Dandelion discovers that the pair are an alien princess and her bodyguard, she guesses L'Lihdra is the princess. In fact, she guesses wrong. L'Lihdra is the bodyguard and Wade is royalty. Her real name is Princess Androuthenyss.

L'Lihdra contains similarities to "lily," a flower of resurrection, and "libra," "free." The character epitomizes freedom as she explores the galaxy with her princess and murders unwanted suitors without consequences.

Phil

Phil the Robot has a name that means "love." In fact, he seems to harbor a secret love for someone, likely Dandelion. This name, as well as the emotion, emphasizes his humanity. Like Xander, he's the male heart of the girl-power team.

Wade/Princess Androuthenyss

Wade is a boy's name with water associations. It comes from the same source as the English word, meaning "to go" or "to ford a river." As water is feminine, there's a bit of a gender cross. Like River, Wade has a water name but journeys through space, merging the paired associations.

The longer name sounds royal with far too many syllables for practicality. It contains an "andro," meaning "man," and "the," meaning belief (both in Latin). She is indeed mannish and has too much faith in men – particularly the groupies with whom she instantly falls in love.

X-Men

The X-Men are most known for their superhero names: self-definition by their powers or sometimes by their self-image. While most characters are well-established, from the X-Men to their enemies and allies, Whedon introduces several characters. His comic book run on *Astonishing X-Men* from 2004-2008 continues the franchise, but resets it to some extent, bringing Colossus back from the dead and joining Beast, Emma Frost, Wolverine, Cyclops, and a few others to save the earth, all starring girl power icon Kitty Pryde.

Agent Abigail Brand

In the Biblical story of King David, Abigail brings supplies to David, deterring him from killing her husband. Unfortunately for the X-Men, Abigail Brand of Whedon's newly created S.W.O.R.D. (Sentient World Observation and Response Department) is less demure. She offers help they don't desire as she takes them over and orders them around.

Agent Brand has tattoos on either arm spelling out "Grace" and "Anna" (women's names that ironically mean the same thing). She in fact has some divine grace through her many alien gifts as revealed at the end of Whedon's arc. Who these women were – past lovers, relatives, or part of Brand's own name – is unclear. Still, the name Anne on her arm links her with Buffy's middle name as well as Kitty Pryde's.

"Abigail" means "my father is joyful," emphasizing Brand's loyalty to the patriarchal structure ... a character trait shared by Maggie Walsh and Adelle DeWitt. As an old-fashioned, charming name, it softens the hard edges of her character. At the same time, Abigail has been the name of two American First Ladies – three, counting the character on *The West Wing*, making it a name of leadership and authority as well as one of subservience to the government hierarchy.

Brand is a harsher name, a single stark syllable evoking

the torture and suffering she offers to her enemy. Originally, a brand represented an indelible mark defining someone or something, the personality they will assert in the world, as Brand does in Whedon's new organization. S.W.O.R.D. is of course a carefully-named counterpart of S.H.I.E.L.D. Brand has stamped it with her personality, and it defines her in turn.

As the Agent dramatically reveals near the story's climax, "Brand" is not her name but her superhero identity. She in fact can burn people with her touch. Thus she becomes a brand on others, a guarantee that they can never forget her.

Armor/Hisako Ichiki

Hisako Ichiki may be the first fully Japanese X-Man, with a name to reflect her heritage. Trapped alone with an injured Wolverine, he offers her a choice – become an X-Man as he believes she can or give up and die. She proudly names herself "Armor." Her red psionic exoskeleton body armor, composed of ancestral memory, protects her from nearly everything and also grants her superhuman strength and durability. With it, she can create a psionic blast.

Hisako means "child of an old story" in Japanese or may be written with characters for "longevity" or "congratulations." As her power comes from her ancestors, these are logical name meanings for the character. She even earns congratulations, as she's the only new X-Man in Whedon's run.

Ichiki is likely related to "Ichikawa," a Japanese surname that means "marketplace river." This is a common place name throughout Japan, associating Hisako with her ancestral home, from which she gains strength.

Blindfold

Blindfold appears shrouded in fringed shawls as well as the iconic piece of clothing that is her namesake. It's soon revealed that she has no eyes beneath the blindfold she often wears. In X-Men fashion, she compensates with telepathy and premonitions of the future.

She appears separated from those around her, in more than her blindness and jarring method of dress. Her speech pattern is marred, with odd insertions of "please," "thank you," and "pardon." Precognitive, she knows what others will say before the conversation begins. In Whedon's arc, she is knocked unconscious by vicious Cassandra Nova's mental attack, and forced to pass on telepathic messages from others. Disabled and marginalized, as a young Asian woman and a student, she lacks confidence around the X-Men. In all her scenes, she appears unhappy, weighted by the doom she is unable to prevent. Later books reveal that she is broken in truth – her brother Luca, who murdered their mother, stole half of her powers at his death, leaving her "broken." As such, she takes her place beside shattered, gifted River Tam, Drusilla, Rebecca Porter, and other mad girls of Whedon's.

The nameless Blindfold and self-naming Armor represent a split between strength and vulnerability. Blindfold, like Willow or Tara, is the fragile sprit, while Armor proudly labels herself as the fighting force and protector. In fact, while defending Blindfold, Hisako's armor expands enormously, vanquishing the attackers with pure ancestral force. While Blindfold is a victim of her family, Hisako's family is her source of strength. By the end of Whedon's arc, Hisako has grown from student to X-Man, while Blindfold remains home, conveying others messages and aiding their destinies.

Kavita Rao

This character, invented by Whedon as the discoverer of the mutant "cure," was picked up by the *X-Men 3* movie that followed, along with her story arc. She also shares a name with River's teacher in *Serenity:* both women are acting unilaterally to help ban those who are different with a goal of the greater good. With her bindi, Rao establishes herself as a figure of organized religion as well, an area Whedon often links with cruelty for the greater good.

"Rao" means king in India, reinforcing that both doctors are part of the establishment, the opposite side from the story's heroes. "Kavita" is Sanskrit for poem or poetry, though the "art" she creates in fact casts the superheroes into turmoil..

> Dr. Kavita Rao's family name resonates with Superman's Silver Age exclamation: "Great Rao!" "Rao" is the name of the pre-eminent sun deity of Superman's native Kryptonian culture making Kavita Rao herself an intertext to the very origin and central defining figure of the superhero genre, Superman ... Just as gods like Rao give a spiritual or metaphysical "hope" to those who worship them, Rao provides the mutants of the Marvel Universe a cure called – appropriately but also ironically – "Hope." (Tony)

If Whedon is referencing Superman, he's flipping and inverting the force of superhero power into the force that confiscates and forbids it. "If Rao is the god that Superman (more or less, traditionally if not literally) attributes his existence to or that gives his life metaphysical meaning, then Dr. Kavita Rao is the god figure that *changes* the meaning of existence for the X-Men and mutants" (Tony). Not one to pull his punches, Whedon invents the cure and alters the nature of the X-Men forever.

Movies

Alien: Resurrection

Whedon's original script for the *Alien* franchise was picked up, resulting in a fourth film with Ripley returning from the dead and battling the aliens once more. A team from the salvage ship the Betty is the only hope, even as the monsters threaten earth.

Annalee Call

The robots from the previous movies had A and B names...she is C. Thus she seems something of an unoriginal product off the shelf, the "Mark C" rather than A. However, her dehumanized name covers a burning ethical nature.

While she's known as Call, her first name combines "Anna" – related to Buffy Anne or Anya and meaning "grace" and "Lee," meaning meadow and anticipating Kaylee's middle name (and Whedon's mother's first name). Thus she connects with Whedon's other girl-power nature goddess women even as she works computer miracles to save the team with a "grace" they don't deserve.

She is also a woman who has "heard the call," that humanity needs saving, thus she becomes Christ figure and martyr. "Her very name, Call, implies that she is a woman with a mission long before the meddling that demonstrates what that is (Kaveney, *Alien to the Matrix* 195). If Ripley is the warrior woman, Call is the sensitive listener attuned to the cosmos – River who calls herself an embodiment of the ship. Like River, Call is both sacrificed woman and young savior. "Call shares with Ripley (and Whedon's Buffy) a capacity to die and be reborn and save her people; her apparent death involves arms outstretched as in a crucifixion" (Kaveney, *Alien to the Matrix* 195).

Betty and Auriga
Ships are "she" and *Betty* has a casual, friendly name. It's a variant on the powerful Elizabeth, and also related to butt-kicking Buffy. It saves them all in the end. By contrast, the original government ship on which Ripley returns, the *Auriga,* is named for a classic constellation, which in turn is named for a male Greek hero. The government is in service to old classical values, which is why the ship is destroyed. Only the spunky *Betty* survives.

Captain Frank Elgyn
Elgyn was a British explorer, namesake of the Elgyn marble statues he brought back with him. He, like his namesake, is more opportunist than hero and unapologetically frank.

Johner
Johner appears a more exotic form of John, the most common, basic male name. Johner is very much a basic, unenlightened male as he makes crude jokes and tries to intimidate Ripley on the basketball court. To him, powerful females are a threat. In many ways, he's a prototype for the similarly-named Jayne, part of a misfit salvage team determined to make a profit, even as the government unleashes terrible monstrosities.

St. Just
An Asian assassin called St. Just was part of the Betty's crew in Whedon's original script. In history, St. Just was one of the leaders of the French Revolution and its Reign of Terror, dubbed the "Angel of Death." The Betty's St. Just, a revolutionary not part of the establishment, may echo him.

According to Whedon's *Tales of the Slayers,* the historical St. Just was a brutal vampire.

Doctor Williamson
This member of Ripley's cloning team is female, but her last name suggests a patriarchal orientation. She is one more in a series of Whedon's Williams.

Doctor Wren
Wren leads the scientists in cloning an alien-Ripley hybrid in an example of body horror and medical horror that Whedon excels in. He's analogous to Doctor Sparrow who "upgrades" Gunn for Wolfram and Hart. Though the bird, like the profession of doctor, seems harmless, he's in fact an amoral monstrosity.

The Cabin in the Woods
Five teens drive to a cabin deep in the woods and awaken the ancient evil there. Everything that follows is a stack of horror clichés, as the film addresses the nature of evil and the prosaic administrators who perpetuate the system.

Curt Vaughan
Curt is short for Conrad, a manly name meaning "brave, bold ruler or counsel." Of course, Curt itself is a manly name, with a short hard syllable meaning short and brusque of speech. As such, it's perfectly suited for the "jock" stereotype.

Vaughan is a Welsh surname meaning small or short. Amongst the many notable bearers of the surname was Richard Vaughan, solicitor to Queen Elizabeth I in 1580, suggesting class and privilege. Another is the poet Henry Vaughan (1622-1695), whose collected poems, entitled "The Retreat," inspired Wordsworth's "Ode on the Intimations of Immortality":

> Happy those early days! when I
> Shined in my angel-infancy,
> Before I understood this place

Appointed for my second race,
Or taught my soul to fancy ought
But a white, celestial thought;
When yet I had not walked above
A mile or two from my first love,
And looking back – at that short space –
Could see a glimpse of His bright face;
When on some gilded cloud, or flower,
My gazing soul would dwell an hour,
And in those weaker glories spy
Some shadows of eternity;
Before I taught my tongue to wound
My conscience with a sinful sound,
Or had the black art to dispense
A several sin to every sense,
But felt through all this fleshy dress
Bright shoots of everlastingness.
    Oh how I long to travel back,
And tread again that ancient track!
That I might once more reach that plain,
Where first I left my glorious train;
From whence the enlightened spirit sees
That shady city of palm trees.
But ah! my soul with too much stay
Is drunk, and staggers in the way.
Some men a forward motion love,
But I by backward steps would move
And when this dust falls to the urn,
In that state I came, return.

In the poem, Vaughan expresses how he does not want to die, even with a beautiful paradise awaiting. As such, this reflects his fated death in *Cabin*.

Dana Polk

Dana is named for the Celtic Danu. This land or water goddess was the land of Ireland, also lending her name to the river Danube. Her identity as mother goddess suggests a similar connotation to Eve – that she is the founding mother of a new world (made literally true by the end).

In Persian, the word literally means "knowledgeable." In Hebrew, the name Dana, related to Daniel, means "God is my judge." A subtle meaning could be that only God should judge her, not the bureaucratic scientists who have condemned her to torture and possible death. In fact, Dana becomes the arbiter of all mankind's fate, in the end.

Dana is an androgynous name, appearing across the world among men and women. Famous Danas include Dana Scully, the sceptic from the *X-Files* and Dana Barrett, featured in the *Ghostbusters* movies, played by actress Sigourney Weaver. (This last may be an homage, as Sigourney Weaver appears in this film as well.) While both characters are possessed and used by supernatural forces, they remain defiant and independent, clear examples of girl power in a man's world of ghosts and alien battles. Dana, of course, is the movie's Final Girl, and her androgynous name emphasizes her role as hero and heroine. As horror expert Carol Clover describes the Final Girl, "She is feminine enough to act out in a gratifying way, a way unapproved for adult males, the terror and masochistic pleasures of the underlying fantasy, but not so feminine so as to disturb the structures of male competence and sexuality" (51). Here is Dana's classic role.

On *Angel,* the girl Dana is driven mad from abuse (in "Damage," A5.11) and then is granted the Slayer power. Thus she becomes strong enough to take revenge not only on her tormenters but on all men, whom she sees as scapegoats. *Cabin*'s Dana, after two hours of torture, likewise condemns the innocent as well as the guilty, once she realizes she has the power to end the world.

Polk derives from "Polska," meaning "the man from Poland." "The origin is Slavonic and is a shortened form of 'Bole,' meaning 'great' and 'slav,' glory, the surname being very popular not surprisingly amongst the ruling classes of the Silesian region, during the medieval period" (SurnameDB). While the name is less "unusual" than Marty Mikalski's name (Polk was a U.S. president after all), the two characters are linked through their Polish heritages. While in U.S. history, British origins were considered more mainstream and privileged than Eastern European ones, it is the two Polish-descended characters who survive and must determine the world's fate.

Holden McCrea

Holden is very much the everyman character, named (presumably) for the famed Holden Caulfield, hero of *Catcher in the Rye.* Both are on the football team, both are students, both have roommates who do better with girls than they do (the girls fall for their friends the jocks, rather than them, the nice guys). There's a similarly self-aware "nice guy" on *Buffy* – vampire Holden Webster in "Conversations with Dead People" (B7.7).

Holden Caulfield's former and much-admired English teacher, Mr. Antolini, quoting a psychologist named Wilhelm Stegel, advises Holden that "The mark of the immature man is that he wants to die nobly for a cause, while the mark of the mature man is that he wants to live humbly for one." In other words, it's better to live and uphold goodness instead of dying for it. This could be a theme of the movie, as Dana and Marty are ordered to die at movie's end but flatly refuse to make the noble sacrifice and perpetuate the system. By living, they take a stand, though ironically it's against humanity.

Holden Caulfield believes that he must be the "catcher in the rye," saving children in his dream from falling off the edge and losing their innocence. He is a protector of the children exploited by adults, while Whedon's teens are an example of those children that need saving as the adults' world threatens to wipe them out. Ironically, in *Cabin*, Holden's job is to die in order to save the world's innocents, and he does. Many say Holden Caulfield does not mature or learn lessons from his adventures in the novel. If Whedon's Holden learns anything, it's undisclosed, as he's stabbed halfway through.

One of the first to die, Holden ironically has a last name, McCrea, that's Scottish for son of grace, prosperity, or favor. It's only a few letters off from Maclay, last name of Tara, who is also fated to die as "collateral damage" in a greater war.

Jules Louden

The name is androgynous, or more precisely masculine, as the French form of the Latin "Julius" (for Julius Caesar). Jules Verne is a namesake. Before Caesar, it may have derived from Greek ἴουλος (*ioulos*) "downy-[haired, bearded]" or the Roman god Jupiter. Both names only add to the masculine image. Listed among Whedon's gender-swapped names, it suggests that Jules is not entirely the girlish victim she's cast as – like Jayne Cobb, she's more than her stereotype.

Of course, Jules sounds like jewels, labeling her as a possession of great beauty and desirability, a gem rather than a person. As such, she fits with the "whore" label, with her virtue barterable for riches.

Her last name Louden is smoothly feminine sounding, like music. While it's not first-letter alliterative, Jules and Louden share vowels, making a name that flows as smoothly as the river of its namesake, contrasted with the sharper Curt or Marty Mikalski. It's a Scottish or English place name, for the town of Loddon, meaning "the dweller by the muddy river." The river is a feminine symbol, and Jules is the most feminine of the characters, before she is sacrificed first.

Marty Mikalski

Marty is the conspiracy theorist and pot smoker. The meaning of the name Marty is "servant of Mars, god of war." Of course, he has the opportunity to sacrifice himself and save the world, but instead lets it descend into chaos – the war god's dream.

If Marty is the Fool archetype, he may be named for comedy actor Marty Feldman or Marty McFly, fictional hero of the *Back to the Future* trilogy.

His last name Mikalski is of Polish origin. It's a less-typical American name than Polk or Vaughan, emphasizing his status as outsider in the group. In their circle of friends or planned double-date, he is left on the outside, to provide witty commentary. Though his humble name Marty suggests a laid-back character, his last name is unusual and ethnic. It's also alliterative, making him sound a bit humorous like Willy Wonka but also subtly setting him in a world of superheroes, where such names are most popular.

Mikalski is derived from the Medieval English personal name "Michael," from the Biblical "Micha-el," "Who is like God?" "The surname also contains the ending "-ski," which in Poland signifies gentry status, and the bearer may also have been the lord of the estate or manor to which the name referred" (Surname DB). It thus means "lordly son of the archangel Michael" a fitting character to end the world. After all, Michael was the leader of God's army, foretold general against the antichrist at the end of days.

The Director
This nameless figure has an imposing title like the Master from *Buffy*. Notably, she's a woman, played by Sigourney Weaver, who played a similar gender-crossing role in the *Alien* franchise. If a soulless corporate evil is destined to bring down the world, she has an aptly chosen title.

Patience and the "Redneck Zombie" Buckners
Patience is a meek Puritan name...though *Firefly*'s Patience is an aggressive frontierswoman, this little girl appears obedient to her family's dictates, then to being a zombie pawn fulfilling her role. Buckner derives from the Old English for a male goat or deer, suggesting a rural strength, speed or sturdiness. With both animals, there's also an association with sacrifice.

Doctor Horrible's Sing-Along Blog
Doctor Horrible is working to take over the world, which is filled with superheroes like oh-so-perfect Captain Hammer. Whedon sums up the plot as follows: "It's the story of Dr. Horrible, a low-rent super villain trying to make his way in the world, being evil, defeat his nemesis, Captain Hammer, who beats him up on a weekly basis, and

work up the courage to talk to the prettiest girl walking around" (qtd. in Leonard 275). It's a parody from beginning to end, as the villain is far more sympathetic than the hero. It's also a video blog, musical, and internet sensation.

Captain Hammer

"In the song 'A Man's Gotta Do,' Captain Hammer (played by Nathan Fillion) is introduced, a muscular man wearing cargo pants, black gloves, and a close-fitting, short-sleeved T-shirt with a hammer on the chest" (Leonard 279). Ironically, the captain's emblem isn't a war hammer, but a simple hand tool for his "corporate tool" status.

Captain Hammer's name suggests chauvinism, like other phallic Whedon characters with matching names (*Dollhouse*'s Alpha, *Buffy*'s Jack O'Toole). All of these dismiss women as objects and are ruled by impulse and violence. Some, like Alpha and Spike, evolve into more balanced and caring individuals, working to help Echo and Buffy respectively. Other chauvinistic characters, from the Master and the Judge of early *Buffy* to Preacher Caleb of the last season (played by Nathan Fillion, like Captain Hammer) are killed by Buffy as she gains empowerment. Based on Whedon's tropes, one of the two outcomes for Captain Hammer is likely if a sequel appears.

Doctor Horrible/Billy

Doctor Horrible himself is reminiscent of the trio that proclaim themselves Buffy's "nemesises" in her sixth season. As he builds gadgets in his basement like they do, a collection of action figures or comic books wouldn't be surprising. He already has a blog after all. His catchphrase, "I've got a Ph.D in Horribleness," emphasizes his agenda, but in fact, he's horrible at being horrible, as he turns gold bars into cuminlike sludge and his freeze ray unfreezes at inopportune moments.

His alter-ego is the helpless Billy, caught in a juvenile crush. His childish, human name signals approachability, in contrast with pompous Captain Hammer. As Billy, the character not only dresses differently but behaves meekly:

> Billy is depicted in traditionally feminine spheres: doing the laundry, blogging from the kitchen (here two traditionally feminine areas overlap: that of communication and speech and that of the kitchen), and sharing frozen yogurt with his crush, Penny, played by Felicia Day. The musical numbers assigned to Billy are also "feminized" in relation to those sung when he is in the guise of Dr. Horrible through use of musical styles commonly regarded as gendered. His first song, which begins when he is in Dr. Horrible garb answering fan e-mail on his blog, instead primarily features Billy in street clothes, singing in a light tenor. (Leonard 278)

As he gushes with Penny, abandoning his tough supervillain persona, he emphasizes his vulnerability.

While Billy means "resolute protector," his ideas for saving the earth are grandiose, vain, and impractical. He fails to save Penny several times, obsessed as he is with his plans and misaligned gadgets. By the end of the movie, he's still childlike, never to grow into "William" as Spike does.

Moist
Moist, Doctor Horrible's henchman, is nicknamed for his power, the ability to make things wet. Dr. Horrible calls him "my evil moisture buddy." As Moist sings in *Commentary! The Musical*:

> Nobody wants to be moist.
> A bunch of overactive pores.
> I struggle opening doors,
> And I lose every tug of war

In the comic *Moist: Humidity Rising,* Moist meets Doctor Horrible and joins the Henchmen's Union so they can work together. It also reveals his origin story as a plutonium-powered humidifier makes him soggy forever.

Penny

Penny is a simple girl from common origins, as suggested by her name. It is, of course, the lowest denomination of coin in America and elsewhere. Characters with the name Penny tend to be children (*Inspector Gadget, Bolt*) or naive young women (*Hairspray, The Big Bang Theory*). "Penny" is a juvenile diminutization of Penelope, the Greek good wife who spends the entire *Odyssey* dodging aggressive suitors and waiting for her husband's return. This Penny seems a good match for the adolescent-seeming Billy, but also a good candidate to become a victim of the patriarchy, a prize to be fought over like her Greek namesake.

As Penny became a helpless victim of men's power games, rather like Tara on *Buffy*, the next female on the scene may be a far stronger supervillain or heroine, like Willow or Dark Willow, determined to teach these immature boys a lesson. She would provide a fitting shadow for Penny and a forceful lesson that Horrible and Hammer need to think about whom they hurt.

In Your Eyes

A young man and woman on opposite sides of the U.S. hear each other's voices in their heads and slowly fall in love, while each encouraging the other to reach their full potential. This film, written by Whedon in 1992 and finally filmed and released on the web in 2014, is sweet and simplistic, exploring the meaning of connection in a classic romantic comedy.

Bellwether Pictures

Joss Whedon and Kai Cole co-created this studio, which produced *Much Ado About Nothing* and *In Your Eyes,* with more projects to come. A bellwether was originally the bell-wearing ram (a wether) that led the sheep, and as a word, it's come to mean trendsetter or groundbreaking leader. One hopes Whedon had the latter definition in mind instead of the former.

Dylan Kershaw

This Welsh name means "son of the sea" – he's also a mythic folk hero. In the *Mabinogion*, Dylan is born to a virgin and dives straight into the sea, already an expert swimmer. As such, Dylan Kershaw becomes a demigod, the perfect romantic hero. He shares a name with poets and singers (Dylan Thomas and Bob Dylan) and appears in every way the perfect guy. His last name is a British one, meaning "church-wood," suggesting a closeness to the land and his community.

Phillip Porter

Phil, as he's most often known, ironically means love. He does appear to love his wife Rebecca, but it's a restrictive, condescending, father-knows-best relationship. He's another of Whedon's evil doctors, echoing Dr. Philbert Mathias who strips River Tam's brain.

Porter, an upper-class Old French name, means "gatekeeper." It's incredibly fitting for Phil, the keeper of the literal gate as he locks Rebecca away and forbids her to leave the institution. He's also the block on her family photos, friendships, and independence. When the names are combined, he's the gatekeeper of love, the reason Rebecca can't be with Dylan.

Rebecca Porter

Her name is flexible of course – her husband calls her Becky in close moments, and Rebecca more formally, while Dylan is soon calling her "Becky" and "Darlin'." It may be significant that Becky sounds like Buffy – back in 1992, the seeds of both gifted young women were percolating. "Rebecca" means "to bind" – fitting as this is a film about connection. Biblical Rebecca bound Isaac to her and was also one of the very few Biblical women to speak with God and receive answers. Thus Biblical Rebecca and Becky Porter both speak to the emptiness in times of doubt, and the emptiness answers back.

Soames Brothers

Soames is one of the earliest of all surnames recorded anywhere, referencing a village called Soham in the county of Cambridgeshire. The "Soames Brothers" are primitive and violent, appealing to Dylan's worst nature as they urge him to return to crime. Their simple rough trade names, Bo and Lyle, would fit easily into a Western as the villain's thugs.

Unmade Films

Afterlife

Afterlife (sold but never filmed) stars scientist Daniel Hofstetter reborn in the body of serial killer Jaime Snows. He goes searching for his wife Laura as the serial killer slowly takes him over (Havens 128, Lavery 83-84). This script offers another Daniel, forced like *Dollhouse*'s Alpha to arbitrate over the war of personality and body. His last name comes from the German for estate-worker and casts him as the guardian of the home, metaphor for the body.

Jaime is a diminutive, making him sound friendly and harmless in contrast with his true nature. It's short for James, he who supplants, suggesting Jaime will begin to take over Daniel's personality. His last name Snow, created long before *Game of Thrones* or *The Hunger Games* gained prominence, suggests the icy chill of amoral murder in contrast with Whedon's many pleasant flower names.

The most famous literary Laura is the muse of Petrarch's sonnets – an object of courtly love and guide for the humble poet much as Beatrice is for Dante. Laura is likely Daniel's spiritual guide as well as his final reward – like the laurel garland of her name's meaning.

Goners

Goners is a fantasy thriller that Whedon described as "like *Buffy*, but scary" (Taylor). Mia, the star, encounters horror in the real world but combats it with a growing strength, much like Whedon's other action heroines. Her name suggests "me," the everygirl, along with the increasingly confident and powerful Mia, heroine of *The Princess Diaries.* Whedon remains cautiously optimistic that it may still be made: "There has been some talk about, after *The Avengers,* trying to resurrect it. I'm not sure what that process would be like" (Taylor).

Suspension

Whedon's *Suspension* is a *Die-Hard*-style story like *Speed,* with terrorists snatching control of New York's George Washington Bridge (Lavery 83). It stars ex-cop Harry Monk, whose religious name (oddly for Whedon) suggests goodness and a drive to protect people. He parallels in first and last names with *Speed's* Harry Temple and may share much of his personality.

Naming Patterns

Repeat Names

- Willow/William Pratt/Liam/Ben Wilkinson/Richard Wilkins III/Carl William Kraft/Billy (*Doctor Horrible*) Also Billy Fordham ("Lie to Me"), Billy Palmer ("Nightmares"), Billy Crandal ("I Only Have Eyes For You"), Billy ("Billy"), Billy Lane (*Welcome to the Team*), Willy the Snitch, Dr. Williamson (*Alien*)
- Anne Pratt/Anya Jenkins/Buffy Anne Summers/Kitty Anne Pryde/Anne Steele ("Anne")/Anaheed/Annalee Call (*Alien*)
- Katrina ("Dead Things")/Kaylee (Firefly)/Kitty Pryde (X-Men)/Kate Lockley/Kathy Newman/ Kitty Fantastico
- Daniel Holtz/Dana Polk/Daniel Osborne/Willow Danielle Rosenberg/Daniel Perrin ("The Left Hand")/ Daniel Hofstetter (*Afterlife*)
- Elizabeth "Buffy" Summers/Beth Maclay/Elizabeth the bug/Betta George/Betty (*Alien*)/Becky Porter
- Jayne Cobb/Johner/Joan ("Tabula Rasa")/Jonathan Levinson
- April/Melinda Mae/November/ *Satsuki* (the month of May)
- Rupert Giles/Robin Wood/ Robert Flutie/Robert Dowling
- Carl William Craft/Charles Gunn/Caroline Farrell/Caroline Holtz
- Lillie (*Runaways*), Lily ("Anne"), L'Lihdra (*Sugarshock*)
- Laurence Dominic/Laura Kay Weathermill/Laura Hofstetter (*Afterlife*)

- Jemma Simmons/Simon Tam/Simone Doppler
- St. Just (original script *Alien: Resurrection*)/St. Just (*Tales of the Slayers*)/Justine (*Angel*)
- Gwen Raiden (Power Play)/Gwendolyn Post ("Revelations")/ Gwen Ditchik ("Inca Mummy Girl")
- Phil Porter (*In Your Eyes*)/Phil Coulson/Phil the robot (*Sugarshock*)/ Dr. Philbert Mathias
- Allen Francis Doyle/Zoe Alleyne Washburne/Alonna Gunn
- Patience (F1.1)/Patience (*Cabin*)/ Patience (A4.21)
- Cecily/Sheila Rosenberg
- Ben Wilkinson/Bennett Halverson
- Holden McCre/Tara Maclay
- Xander/Doctor Saunders
- Spike/Pike
- Holden McCrea/Holden Webster
- Roger Burkle/ Roger Wyndam-Pryce
- Mal Reynolds/Mel Fray
- William Pratt/Klara Prast
- Melaka Fray/Kaylee Frye
- Laura Kay/Kaylee
- Kaylee/Annalee
- Dana (*Cabin*)/Dana ("Damages")
- Adelle DeWitt/Adelai Niska
- Klara (*Runaways*)/Claire Saunders (*Dollhouse*)
- Charles Gunn/Eddie Gunman (*Runaways*)
- Wing ("Shindig")/Wing (*X-Men*)
- Jules Louden/ Jemma Simmons
- Kiki La Rue ("Ariel")/ Kiki ("Belle Chose")
- Melaka/Illyria
- Sierra/Inara Serra
- Marty Mikalski/Marcus Hamilton
- Antoine Triplett/Anthony Ceccoli
- Victor (*Dollhouse*)/Viktor (works for Niska)
- Dr. Mathias/Matthias Pavayne
- Doctor Sparrow (*Angel*)/Doctor Wren (*Alien*)

Bible Names
Simon Tam, Paul Ballard, Luke, Angel, Drusilla, Adam, Caleb, Eve, Parker Abrams, David Nabbitt, Zoe Washburne, Gabriel Tam, Abigail Brand, Dr. Mathias, Jubal Early, Daniel Holtz, Daniel Osborne, Daniel Perrin, Daniel Hofstetter, Willow Danielle Rosenberg, Matthias Pavayne, Jamaerah, Black Maria, Rebecca Porter

Word Names
Faith, Angel, Spike, Whistler, Curt, Patience, Pike, Glory, Tumble, Perfect Jheung, Penny, Radiant Cobb, Call, Serenity, Harmony, Fantastic Rample, Atherton Wing, Stitch Hessian, India Cohen

Nature Names
River, Dawn, Willow, Tara (earth), Maclay (earth), Robin Wood, Vi (Violet), Pomegranate, Xin Rong,, Sierra, Skye, Lillie, Lily, Rosenberg, Summers, Ivy, Iris, Forget-Me-Not, Dandelion, Jasmine, Saffron, Wade, Badger, Wing, Crow, Doctor Sparrow, Doctor Wren, Professor Duck, Jaime Snows

Superhero Names and Designations
The Master, The Judge, The Beast, The Immortal, The Siphon, Twilight, Doctor Horrible, Captain Hammer, Moist, Bad Horse, Armor, Abigail Brand, Blindfold, Whiskey, Alpha, November, Echo, Zone, The Witchbreaker, Maneater, Forget-Me-Not, Spieler, Hoyden, Professor Duck, The Swell, Mr. Universe, The Director, Arcane, Crow, Badger

Word Surnames
Topher Brink, Cordelia Chase, Derrial Book, Charles Gunn, Eddie Gunman, Laura Kay Weathermill, Jubal Early, Holland Manners, Kendra Young, Kathy Newman, Rebecca and Phil Porter, Harry Monk

Alliterative
Cordelia Chase, Melinda May, Marty Mikalski

Literature
Regan Tam, Holden McCrea, Holden Webster, Rossum, Illyria, Lenore, Justine Cooper, Desdemona, Mingojerry Rample, the Difference Engine, Mia, Laura Hofstetter (*Afterlife*)

History
Joan, Kennedy, Alexander, Leopold, Ripper, Jules (Julius), Marcus, Frank Elgyn, St. Just

Myth Names
Tara, Echo, Inara, Illyria, Lilah Morgan, Connor, Harmony, Janna of the Kalderash, Anaheed, Icarus, Erin, Gwen Raiden, Galahad, Saga Vasuki, Iris, Polyphemus, Drogyn, Aphrodesia, Dylan, Tristan, Anya (Áine), Auriga

Ethnic Names
Japanese: Satsu, Hisako Ichiki, Dandelion Naizen
Chinese: Chao-Ahn, Xin Rong, Qiaolian (May's middle name)
Polish: Dana Polk, Marty Mikalski
Czech: Adelai Niska
Romany: Janna of the Kalderash
Jewish: Jonathan Levinson, Willow Rosenberg, India Cohen
French: Genevieve, Roche, Perrin, Bea, Hope Lyonne, Antoine Triplett, St. Just
Greek and Roman: Zoe Alleyne, Laurence Dominic, Iris, Polyphemus, Jules (Julius), Alexander, Kakistos, Marcus Hamilton, Quentin Travers, Auriga
German: Stitch Hessian, Rupert, Garrett, Hofstetter
Italian: Anthony Ceccoli
Indian: Priya Tsetsang, Professor Kavita Rao, Saga Vasuki, Tara
Middle East: Mesekhtet, Sahjhan, Anaheed

British Names

Giles, Wesley Wyndam-Pryce, Tara Maclay, Connor, Allen Francis Doyle, Riley Finn, Laura Kay Weathermill, Holden McCrea, Holland, Kendra, Jules Louden, Curt Vaughan, Kate Lockley, Jemma Simmons, Leo Fitz, Lindsey McDonald, Boyd Langdon, Bennett Halverson, Anya Jenkins, Maggie Walsh, Justine Cooper, Gavin Park, Quentin Travers, Linwood Murrow, Lillie McGurty, Clyde Randolph, Sierra, Atherton Wing, India, Dylan Kershaw, Frank Elgyn

Made-up Names

Lothos (*Buffy* movie)
Kakistos (*Buffy*)
Halfrek (*Buffy*)
Krevlorneswath of the Deathwok Clan (*Angel*)
Mesekhtet (*Angel*)
Sahjhan (*Angel*)
Kaywinnet (*Firefly*)
L'Lihdra (*Sugarshock*)
Androuthenyss (*Sugarshock*)
Johner (*Alien: Resurrection*)

Nicknames

Topher, Xander, Leo, Fitz-Simmons, Mal Reynolds, Kaylee, Wash, Badger, Bea, Fanty, Mingo, Will Rosenberg, Mel Fray, Oz, Tumble, Dez, Rack, Vi, Trip, Flowers, Mag, Zone

First Names for Surnames

Rupert Giles, Zoe Alleyne, Fred Burkle, Dandelion Naizen, Inara Serra, Dr. Mathias, Amy Madison, Parker Abrams, Ben Wilkinson, Clyde Randolph, Laurence Dominic, Mike Peterson, Audrey Nathan

Surnames for First Names

Grant Ward, Kennedy, Hoban, Wade, Bennett, Harth, Holland Manners, Linwood Murrow, Parker Abrams, Atherton Wing,

Girls' Names for Boys
Angel, Lindsey, Cordelia the Dragon, Jayne, Adelai Niska, Tracey Smith, Betta George, Terry Marion Karrens (D2.3)

Boys' Names for Girls
Wade, Dana Polk, Fred, Jules, Bennett, Will Rosenberg, Mel Fray, Audrey Nathan

Whedon's Projects

Title	Credit	Date
TELEVISION		
Buffy the Vampire Slayer	Writer/director /executive producer	1997-2003
Unaired Pilot	Writer	
"Welcome to the Hellmouth"	Writer	10-Mar-97
"The Harvest"	Writer	10-Mar-97
"Nightmares"	Story (teleplay by David Greenwalt)	12-May-97
"Out of Mind, Out of Sight"	Story (teleplay by Ashley Gable and Thomas A. Swyden)	19-May-97
"Prophecy Girl"	Writer/director	2-Jun-97
"When She Was Bad"	Writer/director	15-Sept-97
"School Hard"	Story (with David Greenwalt, teleplay by David Greenwalt)	29-Sept-97
"Lie to Me"	Writer/director	3-Nov-97
"Ted"	Co-writer (with David Greenwalt)	8-Dec-97
"Innocence"	Writer/director	20-Jan-98
"Becoming (Part 1)"	Writer/director	12-May-98
"Becoming (Part 2)"	Writer/director	19-May-98

"Anne"	Writer/director	29-Sept-98
"Amends"	Writer/director	15-Dec-98
"Doppelgangland"	Writer/director	23-Feb-99
"Graduation Day (Part 1)"	Writer/director	18-May-99
"Graduation Day (Part 2)"	Writer/director	13-July-99
"The Freshman"	Writer/director	5-Oct-99
"Hush"	Writer/director	14-Dec-99
"Who Are You"	Writer/director	29-Feb-00
"Restless"	Writer/director	23-May-00
"Family"	Writer/director	7-Nov-00
"The Body"	Writer/director	27-Feb-01
"The Gift"	Writer/director	22-May-01
"Once More, with Feeling"	Writer/director /composer/lyricist	6-Nov-01
"Lessons"	Writer	24-Sept-02
"Conversations with Dead People"	Co-writer, uncredited (with Jane Espenson and Drew Goddard; Marti Noxon, uncredited)	12-Nov-02
"Chosen"	Writer/director	20-May-03
Angel	Writer/director /executive producer	
"City Of"	Co-writer (with David Greenwalt)/director	5-Oct-99
"I Fall to Pieces"	Story (with David	26-Oct-99

186

	Greenwalt, teleplay by David Greenwalt)	
"Sanctuary"	Co-writer (with Tim Minear)	2-May-00
"Judgment"	Story (with David Greenwalt, teleplay by David Greenwalt)	26-Sept-00
"Untouched"	Director	17-Oct-00
"Happy Anniversary"	Story (with David Greenwalt, teleplay by David Greenwalt)	6-Feb-01
"Waiting in the Wings"	Writer/director	4-Feb-02
"Spin the Bottle"	Writer/director	10-Nov-02
"Conviction"	Writer/director	1-Oct-03
"Smile Time"	Story (with Ben Edlund, teleplay by Ben Edlund)	18-Feb-04
"A Hole in the World"	Writer/director	25-Feb-04
"Not Fade Away"	Co-writer (with Jeffrey Bell)	19-May-04
Firefly	Writer/director /executive producer	
"Serenity"	Writer/director	20-Dec-02
"The Train Job"	Co-writer (with Tim Minear)	20-Sept-02

	/director	
"Our Mrs. Reynolds"	Writer	4-Oct-02
"The Message"	Co-writer (with Tim Minear)	28-July-03
"Objects in Space"	Writer/director	13-Dec-02
Dollhouse	Writer/director /executive producer	
"Echo"	Writer/director	N/A
"Ghost"	Writer/director	13-Feb-09
"Man on the Street"	Writer	20-Mar-09
"Epitaph One"	Story (teleplay by Jed Whedon & Tancharoen)	N/A
"Vows"	Writer/director	25-Sept-09
Agents of S.H.I.E.L.D.	Writer/director /executive producer	2013-
"Pilot"	Writer/director (with Jed Whedon & Tancharoen)	24 Sept 2013
FILM		
Buffy the Vampire Slayer	Writer	1992
The Getaway	Cowriter (uncredited)	1994
Speed	Cowriter (uncredited)	1994
Waterworld	Cowriter (uncredited)	1995
Toy Story	Co-writer	1995
Alien Resurrection	Writer	1997

Titan A.E.	Co-writer	2000
X-Men	Treatment (uncredited)	2000
Atlantis: The Lost Empire	Treatment	2001
Serenity	Writer/director	2005
Thor	Directed the post-credits scene (uncredited)	2011
R. Tam sessions	Writer/director /producer	2005
Dr. Horrible's Sing-Along Blog	Co-creator, executive producer, writer, director, music & lyrics	2008
Commentary! The Musical	Co-creator, executive producer, writer, director, performer, music & lyrics	2008
Captain America: The First Avenger	Co-writer (uncredited)	
Astonishing X-Men: Gifted (Motion Comic)	Writer	2010
Buffy the Vampire Slayer: Season 8 Motion Comic	Writer	2011
Comic-Con Episode IV: A Fan's Hope (Documentary)	Director/ producer	2011
Astonishing X-Men: Dangerous (Motion Comic)	Writer	2012
Astonishing X-Men:	Writer	2012

Torn (Motion Comic)		
Astonishing X-Men: Unstoppable (Motion Comic)	Writer	2012
The Cabin in the Woods	Co-writer/producer	2012
The Avengers	Writer/director	2012
Whedon On Romney	Writer/director	2012
Much Ado About Nothing	Adaptor/director/producer	2013
Captain America: The Winter Soldier	Directed the post-credits scene (uncredited)	2014
In Your Eyes	Writer/ executive producer	2014
The Avengers: Age of Ultron	Writer/director	2015

COMICS

Fray (#1-8)	Writer	2001-2003
Tales Of The Slayers (First Slayer, Righteous & Tales)	Writer/editor	2002
Angel: Long Night's Journey (#1-4)	Writer with Brett Matthews	2002
Tales of The Vampires ("Tales of the Vampires" and "Stacy")	Writer/editor	2003-2004
Buffy: The Origin	Writer of original screenplay	

Astonishing X-Men vol. 3: (#1-24) & Giant Size Astonishing X-Men (#1)	Writer	2004-2008
X-Men: Teamwork (in Giant Size X-Men #3)	Writer	2005
Serenity. Those Left Behind (#1-3)	Writer with Brett Matthews	2005
Some Steves (in Stan Lee Meets The Amazing Spider-Man #1)	Writer	2006
Superman/Batman #26 (p. 20-21)	Writer	2006
Buffy The Vampire Slayer Season Eight: (#1-5, 10, 11, 16-19)	Writer	2007-2011
Always Darkest - Myspace Dark Horse Presents #4	Writer with Scott Allie	2010-2011
Angel After The Fall (#1-17)	Writer with Brian Lynch	2007-2009
Runaways vol. 2 (#25-30)	Writer	2007-2009
Serenity. Better Days (#1-3)	Writer with Brett Matthews	2008
Sugarshock: Don't Be a Viking - Myspace Dark Horse Presents 1-3	Writer	2009
Serenity: The Shepherd's Tale	Writer with Zack Whedon	2010
Buffy The Vampire Slayer Season Nine (#1-2)	Writer with Andrew Chambliss	2011

Buffy The Vampire Slayer Season Eight	Executive Producer	2007-2011.
Buffy The Vampire Slayer Season Nine	Executive Producer	2011-2013
Angel & Faith	Executive Producer	2011-

OTHER TELEVISION

"The Little Sister" "House of Grown-Ups" "Brain-Dead Poets Society" "Chicken Hearts"	Writer (*Roseanne*)	1989
"Fun for Kids" "Small Surprises" "The Plague"	Writer (*Parenthood*)	1990–1991
"Pilot" *Buffy: The Animated Series*	Co-creator, executive producer	2004
"Business School" "Branch Wars"	Director (*The Office*)	2007
"Dream On"	Director (*Glee*)	2010

WRITTEN BUT NOT FILMED

Suspension		
Goners		
Afterlife		
Wonder Woman		
Ripper		

Works Cited

Movies

Alien: Resurrection. 1997. 20th Century Fox, 2007. DVD.

Buffy the Vampire Slayer (movie). 1992. 20th Century Fox, 2001. DVD.

The Cabin in the Woods. 2011. Lions Gate, 2012. DVD.

Dr. Horrible's Sing-Along Blog. Mutant Enemy, 2008. DVD.

In Your Eyes. Bellwether Pictures. 2014. Online. https://vimeo.com/ondemand/inyoureyes

Serenity (Widescreen Edition). 2005. DVD. Los Angeles: Universal Studios 2005

Television

Agents of S.H.I.E.L.D.: Season One. ABC. 2013-2014. Television.

Angel: The Complete First Season. The WB Television Network. 1999-2000. DVD. Los Angeles: 20th Century Fox, 2003.

Angel: The Complete Second Season. The WB Television Network. 2000-2001. DVD. Los Angeles: 20th Century Fox, 2003.

Angel: The Complete Third Season. The WB Television Network. 2001-2002. DVD. Los Angeles: 20th Century Fox, 2004.

Angel: The Complete Fourth Season. The WB Television Network. 2002-2003. DVD. Los Angeles: 20th Century Fox, 2004.

Angel: The Complete Fifth Season. The WB Television Network. 2003-2004. DVD. Los Angeles: 20th Century Fox, 2005.

Buffy the Vampire Slayer: The Complete First Season. The WB Television Network. 1997. DVD. Los Angeles: 20th

Century Fox, 2002.

Buffy the Vampire Slayer: The Complete Second Season. The WB Television Network. 1997-1998. DVD. Los Angeles: 20th Century Fox, 2002.

Buffy the Vampire Slayer: The Complete Third Season. The WB Television Network. 1998-1999. DVD. Los Angeles: 20th Century Fox, 2006.

Buffy the Vampire Slayer: The Complete Fourth Season. 1999-2000. The WB Television Network. DVD. Los Angeles: 20th Century Fox, 2003.

Buffy the Vampire Slayer: The Complete Fifth Season. The WB Television Network. 2000-2001. DVD. Los Angeles: 20th Century Fox, 2006.

Buffy the Vampire Slayer: The Complete Sixth Season. UPN. 2001-2002. DVD. Los Angeles: 20th Century Fox, 2004.

Buffy the Vampire Slayer: The Complete Seventh Season. UPN. 2002-2003. DVD. Los Angeles: 20th Century Fox, 2008.

Buffy the Vampire Slayer: Season 8 Motion Comic. DVD. Los Angeles: 20th Century Fox, 2011.

Dollhouse: Season One. 2009. DVD. Los Angeles: 20th Century Fox, 2009.

Dollhouse: Season Two. 2009. DVD. Los Angeles: 20th Century Fox, 2010.

Firefly: The Complete Series. 2002. DVD. Los Angeles: 20th Century Fox, 2003.

Comics

Allie, Scott, Sierra Hahn, and others. *Buffy the Vampire Slayer Season 9 Volume 3 Guarded.* OR: Dark Horse, 2013.

Brereton, Dan, and Christopher Golden. "Buffy: The Origin." *Buffy the Vampire Slayer Omnibus: Volume 1.* Milwaukie, OR: Dark Horse, 2007.

Chambliss, Andrew, Scott Allie, Sierra Hahn, and Georges Jeanty. *Buffy the Vampire Slayer Season 9 Volume 2: On Your Own.* OR: Dark Horse, 2012.

Chambliss, Andrew, Sierra Hahn, Scott Allie and others.

Buffy the Vampire Slayer Season 9 Volume 4: Welcome to the Team. OR: Dark Horse, 2013.

Espenson, Jane, and Georges Jeanty. *Predators and Prey*, Season 8, Vol. 5. Milwaukie, OR: Dark Horse, 2009.

Gage, Christos, Lee Garbett, Derek Fridolfs, and Rebekah Isaacs. *Angel & Faith Volume 3: Family Reunion.* OR: Dark Horse, 2013.

Gage, Christos, Scott Allie, Rebekah Isaacs and Phil Noto. *Angel and Faith Volume 1: Live Through This.* OR: Dark Horse, 2012.

Gage, Christos, Scott Allie, and Sierra Hahn. *Angel & Faith Volume 4: Death and Consequences* by OR: Dark Horse, 2013.

Gage, Christos, Sierra Hahn, Scott Allie, and Rebekah Isaacs. *Angel & Faith Volume 2: Daddy Issues.* OR: Dark Horse, 2012.

Gage, Christos, Sierra Hahn, Scott Allie, and Rebekah Isaacs. *Angel & Faith Volume 5: What You Want, Not What You Need.* OR: Dark Horse, 2014.

Goddard, Drew, and Georges Jeanty. *Wolves at the Gate*, Season 8, Vol. 3. Milwaukie, OR: Dark Horse, 2008.

Loeb, Jeph, Joss Whedon, and Karl Moline. *Time of Your Life*, Season 8, Vol. 4. Milwaukie, OR: Dark Horse, 2008.

– . *Retreat*, Season 8, Vol. 6 Milwaukie, OR: Dark Horse, 2010.

Meltzer, Brad, Joss Whedon, Georges Jeanty, and Karl Moline. *Twilight*, Season 8, Vol. 7. Milwaukie, OR: Dark Horse, 2010.

Moline, Karl, Scott Allie, and Sierra Hahn. *Buffy the Vampire Slayer Season Nine Volume 5: The Core.* OR: Dark Horse, 2014.

Vaughan, Brian K., Joss Whedon, and Georges Jeanty. *No Future for You*, Season 8, Vol. 2. Milwaukie, OR: Dark Horse, 2008.

Whedon, Joss. "Long Night's Journey." *Angel Omnibus.* Ed. Scott Allie. OR: Dark Horse, 2011. 388-483.

Whedon, Joss. "Sugarshock." *Dark Horse Presents #1.* OR: Dark Horse, 2008. 5-28.

Whedon, Joss. *Tales of the Slayers* (Buffy the Vampire Slayer) OR: Dark Horse, 2002.

Whedon, Joss, Andrew Chambliss, Sierra Hahn, and Scott Allie. *Buffy the Vampire Slayer: Season Nine vol. 1 Freefall*. OR: Dark Horse, 2012.

Whedon, Joss, Ben Edlund, Jane Espensen and Brett Matthews. *Tales of the Vampires.* OR: Dark Horse, 2004.

Whedon, Joss, Brett Matthews, and Will Conrad. *Serenity, Vol. 1: Those Left Behind.* OR: Dark Horse, 2006.

Whedon, Joss, Brett Matthews, Will Conrad and Adam Hughes. *Serenity, Vol. 2: Better Days and Other Stories.* OR: Dark Horse, 2008.

Whedon, Joss and Georges Jeanty. *The Long Way Home,* Season 8, Vol. 1. Milwaukie, OR: Dark Horse, 2007.

Whedon, Joss, Karl Moline, and Andy Owens. *Fray.* Milwaukie, OR: Dark Horse, 2003.

Whedon, Joss, Jane Espenson, Scott Allie, and Georges Jeanty. *Last Gleaming,* Season 8, Vol. 8. Milwaukie, OR: Dark Horse, 2011.

Whedon, Joss and John Cassaday. *Astonishing X-Men Vol. 1: Gifted.* USA: Marvel, 2006.

Whedon, Joss and John Cassaday. *Astonishing X-Men Vol. 2: Dangerous.* USA: Marvel, 2007.

Whedon, Joss and John Cassaday. *Astonishing X-Men Vol. 3: Torn.* USA: Marvel, 2007.

Whedon, Joss and John Cassaday. *Astonishing X-Men Vol. 4: Unstoppable.* USA: Marvel, 2008.

Whedon, Joss and Michael Ryan. *Runaways, Vol. 8: Dead End Kids.* USA: Marvel, 2009.

Whedon, Joss and Scott Allie. "Always Darkest." *Myspace Dark Horse Presents #4*. OR: Dark Horse, 2009.

Whedon, Zack and Georges Jeanty. *Serenity: Leaves on the Wind* #1-4. OR: Dark Horse 2014

Whedon, Zack, Joss Whedon, Chris Samnee, Dave Stewart, and Steve Morris. *Serenity: The Shepherd's Tale.* OR: Dark Horse, 2010.

Interviews

Bahr, Lindsey, et al. "Marvel's Agents Of S.H.I.E.L.D."
Entertainment Weekly 1277/1278 (2013): 87.
Academic Search Complete.

"Interview with Nathan Fillion" *Dreamwatch Magazine* 107
9 Sept 2003.
http://www.whedon.info/article.php3?id_article=153
1&img=

"Joss to Never Learn..." *Whedonesque.* Blog Post. November
9, 2005. http://whedonesque.com/comments/8735.

"Joss Whedon at Wizard World in Chicago." *City of Angel:
Behind the Scenes* 10 Sept 2000.
http://www.cityofangel.com/behindTheScenes/bts/jo
ss2.html.

Lee, Michael J. "Jewel Staite." *Radio Free Entertainment* 15
Sept 2005.
http://www.radiofree.com/profiles/jewel_staite/inter
view02.shtml.

Taylor, Drew. "SXSW '12: Joss Whedon Talks Challenges of
The Avengers, Potentially Resurrecting Old Horror Epic
Goners, and How *Cabin In The Woods* Came To Be."
IndieWire 10 Mar 2012.
http://blogs.indiewire.com/theplaylist.

Secondary Sources

Anderson, Wendy Love. "Prophecy Girl and the Powers
That Be: The Philosophy of Religion in the Buffyverse."
South 212-226.

Apollodorus. The Library. Translated by Sir James George
Frazer. Loeb Classical Library Volumes 121 & 122.
Cambridge, MA, Harvard University Press; London,
William Heinemann Ltd. 1921.
http://www.theoi.com/Text/Apollodorus3.html

Appellation Mountain. "Echo, Xander, Zoe: Joss Whedon
Baby Names." 8 March 2013.
http://appellationmountain.net/echo-xander-zoe-joss-
whedon-baby-names

Appian's *History of Rome*: The Illyrian Wars §§1-5 Trans.

Horace White. http://www.livius.org/ap-
ark/appian/appian_illyrian_1.html

Beadling, Laura L. "The Threat of the 'Good Wife'" Wilcox
and Cochran 53-62.

Beckman, Gary. "The Anatolian Myth of Illuyanka."
http://www.academia.edu/260643/The_Anatolian_My
th_of_Illuyanka.

Biedermann, Hans. *Dictionary of Symbolism.* Trans, James
Hulbert. USA: Penguin, 1994.

Bourdier, J. Chris. "The Verse in Numbers." Version 2.0.
Universal Studios and Quantum Mechanix, Inc. Nov
2011. http://pics.fireflyprops.net/TVIN-2.0.pdf

Buckman, Alyson R. "Wheel Never Stops Turning." *Reading
Joss Whedon.* Ed. Rhonda V. Wilcox, Tanya R. Cochran,
Cynthea Masson, and David Lavery. New York:
Syracuse University Press 2014. 169-184.

Chevalier, Jean and Alain Gheerbrant. *A Dictionary of
Symbols.* Trans. John Buchanan-Brown. Oxford:
Blackwell, 1994.

Clover, Carol. *Men, Women, and Chainsaws: Gender in the
Modern Horror Film.* Princeton: Princeton University
Press, 1992.

DeCandido, Keith R.A. *Serenity.* New York: Pocket Star
Books, 2005.

"Designing the Perfect Dollhouse." Featurette. *Dollhouse:
Season One.*

Edwards, Lynne Y., Elizabeth L. Rambo, and James B. South.
Buffy Goes Dark: Essays on the Final Two Seasons of
Buffy the Vampire Slayer *on Television.* Jefferson, NC:
McFarland, 2008.

Espenson, Jane. "Introduction." *Finding Serenity: Anti-
heroes, Lost Shepherds and Space Hookers in Joss
Whedon's Firefly.* Ed. Jane Espenson. USA: Smart Pop,
2005. 1-3.

Ferguson, George and George Wells. *Signs & Symbols in
Christian Art.* Oxford: Oxford University Press, 1959.

Francis, Jr., James. "'Selfless': Locating Female Identity in
Anya/Anyanka Through Prostitution." Paper presented

at the Slayage Conference on *Buffy the Vampire Slayer*, Nashville, TN, 27-30 May 2004.

Frankel, Valerie Estelle. "All Dolled Up" *Inside Joss' Dollhouse: From Alpha to Rossum.* Ed. Jane Espenson. USA: Smart Pop, 2010. 63-78

– . *Buffy and the Heroine's Journey.* Jefferson, NC: McFarland and Co., 2012.

Goldberg, Matt. "Interview: Joss Whedon – Dollhouse." *Collider* 6 Feb 2009. http://collider.com/entertainment/interviews/article. asp/aid/10819/tcid/1

Golden, Christopher and Nancy Holder. *Sunnydale High Yearbook.* New York: Pocket Books, 1999.

Golden, Christopher, Stephen R. Bissette and Thomas E. Sniegoski. *Buffy the Vampire Slayer: The Monster Book.* New York: Pocket Books, 2000.

Havens, Candace. *Joss Whedon: The Genius Behind* Buffy. Dallas: BenBella, 2003.

Hawkins, Paul. "Season Six and the Supreme Ordeal." Edwards, Rambo, and South, 183–97.

"House of Names." Swyrich 2014. http://www.houseofnames.com

Jowett, Lorna. *Sex and the Slayer: A Gender Studies Primer for the* Buffy *Fan.* Middletown, CT: Wesleyan University Press, 2005.

Kaveney, Roz. *From Alien to The Matrix: Reading Science Fiction Film.* USA: I. B. Tauris, 2005.

– . "'She Saved the World. A Lot': An Introduction to the Themes and Structures of *Buffy* and *Angel*" Kaveney 1-36.

Koontz, K. Dale. "Czech Mate: Whedon, Čapek, and the Foundations of *Dollhouse*" *Slayage* 8.2 & 8.3 [30 & 31], Summer/Fall 2010 http://slayageonline.com.

– . *Faith and Choice in the Works of Joss Whedon.* Jefferson, NC: McFarland, 2008.

– . "The One That Almost Got Away: Doyle and the Fish Story" *Slayage 26* http://slayageonline.com/essays/slayage26/Koontz.

Lavery, David. *Joss Whedon: A Creative Portrait.* New York: I.B. Tauris, 2014.

Leonard, Kendra Preston. "The Status is not Quo: Gender and Performance in *Doctor Horrible's Sing-Along Blog.*" *Buffy, Ballads, and Bad Guys Who Sing: Music in the Worlds of Joss Whedon.* Ed. Kendra Preston Leonard. Lanham, MD: Scarecrow Press, 2011. 275-292.

Lerner, Neil. "Music, Race, and Paradoxes of Representation in an Episode of *Firefly*: Jubal Early's Musical Motif of Barbarism in 'Objects in Space'" Wilcox and Cochran 184-190.

"Life is the Big Bad – Season Six Overview" Featurette. *Buffy the Vampire Slayer*: The Complete Sixth Season. UPN. 2001-2002. DVD. Los Angeles: 20th Century Fox, 2004.

Lowe, Donna. "The Last Spike: Jungian Individuation In *Buffy The Vampire Slayer.*" *Watcher Junior* Issue 1 July 2006.

McGuire, Seanan. "The Girls Next Door: Learning to Live with the Living Dead and Never Even Break a Nail." *Whedonistas: A Celebration of the Worlds of Joss Whedon by the Women Who Love Them.* Ed. Lynne M. Thomas and Deborah Stanish. Des Moines: Mad Norwegian Books, 2011.

Middleton, Jason. "Buffy as Femme Fatale." *Undead TV: Essays on Buffy the Vampire Slayer.* Elana Levine and Lisa Ann Parks, eds. USA: Duke University Press, 2007. 145-167.

Robinson, Paschal. *The Catholic Encyclopedia.* Vol. 4. New York: Robert Appleton Company, 1908. 5 May 2014. http://www.newadvent.org/cathen/04004a.htm

Satran, Pamela Redmond and Linda Rosenkrantz. *Nameberry.* Nameberry.com 2014.

Shepherd, Rowena and Rupert. *1000 Symbols: What Shapes Mean in Art and Myth.* New York: Thames & Hudson, 2002.

South, James B. ""My God, it's like a Greek tragedy": Willow Rosenberg and Human Irrationality" South 131-145.

South, James B., ed. *"Buffy the Vampire Slayer" and Philosophy: Fear and Trembling in Sunnydale.* USA: Open Court, 2003.

"Spike, Me." Featurette. *Buffy the Vampire Slayer: The Complete Fourth Season.*

Steeves, Richard P. "Wrapped Up Like a Tube Special Presentation – Dollhouse's Topher Brink: Man of Science, or Satan in a Sweater Vest?" *Wrapped Up Like a Blog* 1 Apr 2010. http://richsteeves.blogspot.com.

SurnameDB .com. *The Internet Surname Database.* 2014. http://www.surnamedb.com/Surname.

Tony. "The Secret Origin of Dr. Kavita Rao." *Cosmic Utility Infinity Ring.* 14 Jan 2011. http://cosmicutilityinfinityring.blogspot.com/2011/01/secret-origin-of-dr-kavita-rao.html.

TV Tropes. "Mary Sue" *TV Tropes.* http://tvtropes.org/pmwiki/pmwiki.php/Main/MarySue

Watts, Donald. *Dictionary of Plant Lore.* Oxford: Academic Press, 2007.

Whedon, Joss. *Buffy the Vampire Slayer: The Script Book.* USA; Pocket Books, 2000.

– . *Firefly: The Official Companion: Volume One.* UK: Titan Books, 2006.

– . *Firefly: The Official Companion: Volume Two.* UK: Titan Books, 2006.

– . *Serenity: The Official Visual Companion.* UK: Titan Books, 2005.

Wilcox, Rhonda V. "Echoes of Complicity: Reflexivity and Identity in Joss Whedon's *Dollhouse" Slayage* 30-31. *Slayage* 30-31 (Summer/Fall 2010) http://slayageonline.com/Numbers/slayage30_31.htm

– . "'I Don't Hold to That': Joss Whedon and Original Sin." Wilcox and Cochran 155-166.

– . "Who Died and Made Her the Boss? Patterns of Mortality in *Buffy.*" Wilcox and Lavery, 3-17.

– . *Why Buffy Matters: The Art of Buffy the Vampire Slayer.* New York: I.B. Tauris, 2005.

Wilcox, Rhonda V. and Tanya Cochran. "Introduction,"
Wilcox and Cochran 1-11.

Wilcox, Rhonda V. Wilcox and Tanya R. Cochran, eds.
Investigating Firefly. USA: I.B. Tauris, 2008.

Wilcox, Rhonda V., and David Lavery, eds. *Fighting the
Forces: What's at Stake in* Buffy the Vampire Slayer.
New York: Rowman and Littlefield, 2002.

Index

211

About the Author

Valerie Estelle Frankel is the author of many nonfiction books:

- *Buffy and the Heroine's Journey*
- *From Girl to Goddess: The Heroine's Journey in Myth and Legend*
- *Katniss the Cattail: An Unauthorized Guide to Names and Symbols in The Hunger Games*
- *Winter is Coming: Symbols, Portents, and Hidden Meanings in A Game of Thrones*
- *Winning the Game of Thrones: The Host of Characters and their Agendas*
- *Doctor Who: The What Where and How*
- *Sherlock: Every Canon Reference You May Have Missed in BBC's Series 1-3*
- *Women in Game of Thrones: Power, Conformity, and Resistance*

Once a lecturer at San Jose State University, she's a frequent speaker on fantasy, myth, pop culture, and the heroine's journey and can be found at http://vefrankel.com.

8539254R00126

Printed in Great Britain
by Amazon.co.uk, Ltd.,
Marston Gate.